STEALING WITH THE EYES

WILL BUCKINGHAM is a writer of fiction and non-fiction for adults and children. He has worked at universities in the UK, China and Myanmar, most recently as visiting professor of Humanities at the Parami Institute, Yangon. He is the author of *Sixty-Four Chance Pieces* and *Lucy and the Rocket Dog*.

STEALING WITH THE EYES
Imaginings and Incantations in Indonesia

WILL BUCKINGHAM

Published in 2018 by
HAUS PUBLISHING LTD
4 Cinnamon Row
London SW11 3TW

A CIP catalogue record for this book is available from the British Library

ISBN: 978-1-909961-42-5
eISBN: 978-1-909961-43-2

Typeset in Garamond by MacGuru Ltd

Printed in the UK by TJ International

For the ancestors, with my apologies

CONTENTS

The Indonesian Archipelago

The Tanimbar Islands

Fordata

Labobar

Larat

Wotar

Wuliaru

Selu

Yamdena

Makatian

Alusi Krawain

Alusi Kelaan

Lorwembun

Arui Bab

Sera

Sangliat Dol

Atubul

Tumbur

Wowonda

Latdalam

Sifnana

Olilit

SAUMLAKI

20 miles

Selaru

PART I

BARANG ANEH

STRANGE THINGS

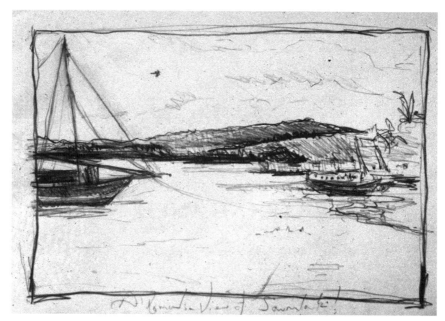

A view of Saumlaki in the Tanimbar Islands

1

AN EXORCISM OF SORTS

I still dream of Tanimbar. I dream of scattered islands and atolls, of rocky bluffs and of cliffs that plunge down into the blue-green water. I dream of fleets of outrigger canoes putting out to sea for sea cucumber. I dream of journeys on foot up the coast roads at night, the stench of forest buffalo hanging in the air. I dream of frigate birds that wheel and circle over my head. I dream of heirloom gold that flashes in the sunlight like the plumage of fighting cocks. And I dream of the sun, shattered into a million parts. These dreams do not come frequently, but when they do I wake with a nagging sense of unease, a mixture of nostalgia and gratitude and regret.

The last time I dreamed of Tanimbar was some months ago. The dream was so vivid that when I woke in the pale light of an English spring morning, my heart beating fast, it took me a few moments to realise where I was. Beached upon the sheets in the morning light, feeling the tides of the dream pull back, I realised that it was twenty years since I had touched down in Saumlaki.

Later that morning, I took down the old cardboard box that sat on top of my bookshelves and opened it up. Inside were sheaves of letters, tattered photocopies, plastic boxes of photographic transparencies. I held up the slides against the light, one by one. The transparencies were turning green with age. Each slide was like a tiny illuminated flash of memory. As I looked through the slides, names and half-remembered Indonesian phrases returned to me. I had a strange sense that I had unfinished business with Tanimbar, or that Tanimbar had unfinished business with me. I had debts to discharge, obligations to meet, even if I was not sure what these debts and obligations were.

I packed the slides away. It was then I realised that after two decades I wanted to write about Tanimbar. I wanted to pass on the stories I had been told, to trade in things half remembered and half forgotten. It would be an exorcism of sorts. It would be what in Tanimbar they call – or they once called – a *mandi adat*, a ritual-law bathing that squares all accounts with the past.

I packed the slides and the photocopies and the letters away. Then I went out into the spring morning to clear my head.

I flew to Tanimbar at the age of twenty-three, a fledgling anthropologist. A few years before, whilst enrolled at university as a somewhat lacklustre student of fine arts, I had stumbled across the anthropology section in the library and I was immediately enchanted. From the very start, what anthropology taught me was that the possibilities for human life were many. Anthropology sang praises to the malleability of human existence. The more I read, the more I came to see that the things I took to be common sense, the things that I believed were *simply the way things were*, were nothing of the sort. Kinship, marriage, ethics, law, religion, life, death, politics – everything that mattered seemed up for grabs. Anthropology was an escape route, a back door by means of which I could slip the net of my own assumptions and beliefs.

So, instead of spending my days in the art studio trying to wrestle with the intractability of paint and canvas, I took to hunting and gathering in the library amongst the anthropology stacks. I read about the Nuer, the Mbuti, the Azande, the Trobrianders, the Ik and the Toraja. And sometime midway through my art degree I decided that, like thousands of anthropologists before me, I too would go out into the field and engage in some ethnography – that curious brand of high-minded intrusiveness amongst peoples too polite, or too powerless, to tell you to go fuck yourself.

I started to make plans. And I came, by degrees, to settle on the Tanimbar Islands, a small archipelago set at the end of the long arm of volcanic islands that stretches from Sumatra to Java to Bali and Lombok to Nusa Tenggara and Timor. There were tantalising suggestions that Tanimbar had strong traditions of carving in wood and stone. I decided I would go to Tanimbar to find out more about these traditions, and to meet the artists who still worked there.

Undaunted by the fact that I had no qualifications in anthropology whatsoever, I wrote a research proposal for the Indonesian Institute of Sciences, and contacted universities in Indonesia to ask if they would work with me. I visited museums in London and in the Netherlands. In dusty storerooms I gazed at beautifully carved house-altars, or *tavu*, adorned with swirling wave patterns; at squatting ancestor figures, or *walut*; and at *kora ulu* prow boards from war canoes, decorated with fighting cocks. Meanwhile, I opened a bank account and started to apply for grants to fund my trip. The money began to trickle in.

Somehow, by the time I graduated from my degree, I found myself with a bundle of permission letters, the backing of the University of Pattimura in Ambon, a permission letter from Lembaga Ilmu Pengetahuan Indonesia – the Indonesian Institute of Sciences – and a small research budget to pay for the trip. All this is how, towards the end of the summer of 1994, I came to catch a flight to Indonesia.

At the heart of the story that follows are my encounters with three remarkable sculptors – Matias Fatruan, Abraham Amelwatin and Damianus Masele. My instructors, guides and accusers, these three men taught me lessons that I am still struggling to fully master. I am indebted to them. But this book is about other things besides. It is about possession and exorcism, sickness and healing, time and history, uncertainty and change. And it is about how I eventually took fright at the prospect of becoming an anthropologist, and how I came to leave behind anthropology – the art, as Matias Fatruan put it, of 'stealing with the eyes' – for good.

2

SHIT-BABY

Getting to the Tanimbar Islands was not easy. It was a late summer afternoon when I boarded the plane to Jakarta. I touched down and found myself a cheap guest room in Jalan Jaksa, where the travellers' hostels were. I spent my first two weeks in Indonesia involved in paperwork. I shuttled between government offices, waited in corridors under slow-turning fans, processing documents and collecting official stamps on my growing stack of permission letters, permits and passes. Eventually it was done and I flew east to Ambon, the provincial capital of Maluku province. In the hotel in Ambon, the receptionist, an attractive woman in her mid-twenties, looked alarmed when I said I was going to Tanimbar.

'There are many witches in Tanimbar,' she said. 'You must be careful.' I could see from the expression on her face that she was not joking. I reassured her that I would take care.

From Ambon – having failed to book a space on the infrequent flight to Saumlaki, the capital of the Tanimbar Islands – I hitched a ride to the volcanic Banda Islands, taking the slow route to Tanimbar. In Banda I gorged on fresh fruit, read and re-read anthropology textbooks and swatted away mosquitoes as I waited for the next ship south. It was a week before the boat arrived – a passenger ship run by the Perintis (meaning 'pioneer') shipping line. The ship had once done service as a Chinese cargo vessel – you could still see the Chinese characters beneath the paint on the hull – but had since been converted into a passenger ship. It now carried up to three hundred passengers on the open deck, sheltered from the elements by an orange tarpaulin.

I spent three sleepless nights on the deck of the boat before we put in to port in Tual, the capital of the Kei Islands. I was tired and dirty, and there were several days of travelling to go until we reached Saumlaki. Not only this, but the mosquito bites I had picked up in Banda had already turned into running sores. I disembarked and bought myself some ointment for my infected bites from a pharmacist. Next to the pharmacy was a travel agency. I went inside and asked about the best way to get to Saumlaki. There was an unscheduled flight from Tual the following morning. I booked myself a ticket.

The following day, I hitched a ride to the airport on the back of a motorbike. The plane arrived – a small twin-prop, built in Indonesia after an Italian design. We flew south-west across the ocean, and then down the coast of Tanimbar's largest island, Yamdena. I could see the road that connected the villages strung out along the seaboard. A couple of vehicles inched along like termites. The villages below me were orderly, their rusting tin and grass roofs extending inland from the beaches in strict rows.

We circled over Saumlaki. Out in the bay, boats were moored along the jetty. The plane banked, the water flashed in the afternoon sun and the ground loomed towards us. There was a blur of treetops followed by the thud of wheels on tarmac. Everybody clapped. My fellow passengers smiled and offered up prayers, to God and to the ancestors.

Saumlaki airport – a couple of miles out of town – was no more than a single-storey building by the side of an airstrip. The plane taxied to a halt and we clambered out. I took my bag and I walked past the sleepy officials, through the arrivals lounge. Outside, a small cluster of mini-buses and taxis was waiting to ferry arrivals into town. The afternoon was sunny but not too hot, a breeze coming off the sea. I clambered into a Suzuki minibus. A neatly dressed man with a small briefcase and a holdall got in behind me and smiled. The driver offered to take me to the Harapan Indah hotel. The name, in translation, meant 'Lovely Hope'. It was the best hotel in town, he told me. There was another hotel, cheaper than the Harapan Indah, but it doubled up as a brothel. 'You will be more comfortable in the Harapan Indah,' he said.

Without waiting to fill any of the remaining seats, the taxi driver pulled away. The road into town was lush with thick vegetation. Cows grazed on the verges. My fellow passenger was chatty. He was a government official from Surabaya in East Java, returning from Ambon where he had been attending some meeting or other. He had lived in Tanimbar a long time.

'Do you like it here?' I asked him.

He hesitated. 'Tanimbar is different,' he said. 'It is different from Ambon and Surabaya. You have to understand the people here. If you understand the people, you will not have any problems. What are you doing here?'

I told him that I had come to study the art of woodcarvers.

He nodded. 'You will find it interesting,' he said. 'There is a lot of history here. *Adat* is very strong.'

'*Adat*' is one of those words that are almost impossible to translate with precision. Usually it is rendered as 'ritual law', which is to say the law sanctioned by the ancestors. In this sense, *adat* involves everything from land rights to whom you can or cannot marry, as well as questions about inheritance, about rituals and about taboos on particular foods. *Adat* is so extensive in its reach that it impinges upon almost all aspects of everyday life. But *adat* is more than just a matter of tradition, ritual or customary practice. I soon came to realise that, for the Tanimbarese, *adat* had all the force of the laws of nature. To break with *adat* was to risk angering the ancestors. A violation could lead to madness, sickness or death.

The Javanese official leaned towards me. 'You must be careful,' he said. 'I have seen many things here in Tanimbar. There are many *barang aneh*.'

Barang aneh: strange things. I had not heard the expression before. But over the months that followed, I became accustomed to talk of *barang aneh*. It was a catch-all category for anomalous events and strange phenomena – uncanny forms of magic, vengeful witches, tetchy ancestors or deranged foreigners.

The minibus pulled into Saumlaki, the lush verges giving way to houses and shops. The Javanese official stared out of the window. Then he called out to the driver, who pulled up to a halt. My fellow passenger jumped out and shook my hand.

'Good luck,' he said, sliding the door closed. It appeared that I was paying for us both.

He waved us off as we headed down Saumlaki's main street. I looked out at the low shops and houses. They were shabby and down at heel. A few moments later the taxi stopped in front of the Harapan Indah. I paid the driver and climbed out. Then I stepped into the hotel.

The reception area was spacious and cool, decorated with woven ikat cloths. Cases of Tanimbarese art made for the tourist trade lined the walls: sculptures carved from *kayu hitam*, or black wood. The sculptures seemed strangely dissimilar to those I had seen in the stores of museums in London, Amsterdam and Leiden.

I rang the bell on the front desk. A friendly, briskly efficient woman in her late twenties came out of the back office.

'Welcome,' she said in English. 'Are you looking for a room?'

This was Dina Go, the hotel manager. The Go family were Chinese-Indonesian merchants who ran a small business empire centred in Saumlaki, trading throughout Tanimbar and beyond. Dina checked me in. I took one of the cheaper rooms upstairs. I dumped my bags, then Dina showed me around. At the back of the hotel, a wooden pontoon stretched out into the bay. The pontoon was crowded with luxuriant pot plants. Across the other side of the water, I could see the low hills. It was a beautiful spot.

'Welcome to Tanimbar,' Dina said. 'I'll get somebody to bring you a drink. Coffee?'

'Coffee would be great,' I said.

I looked out to sea and drank my coffee. The air was becoming cooler as the afternoon advanced. I drained the last dregs, then walked back through the hotel and into the street. Saumlaki was waking up after its afternoon siesta, merchants rolling up the shutters of their shops. I headed down the dusty main street to the Yamdena Plaza, a crumbling concrete complex of small shops selling Chinese-made fountain pens, medicines, expensive snacks, soap, dried fish and cheap hardback notebooks. Outside the pool hall lounged a cluster of bored, unemployed youths. One was seated on a motorised scooter, stripped to the waist, wearing mirror shades.

'*Orang bule*,' he muttered. 'Whitey'. When I passed, I felt a rain of small stones skittering around me. I did not turn round.

The Yamdena Plaza was the commercial heart of the Tanimbar Islands. Barefoot villagers were negotiating prices of sacks of copra with better-dressed merchants. A man lurched towards me carrying a bag of sculptures and ikat cloths.

'Sculptures?' he asked in English. 'Ikat? Very cheap. Dollar price.' I shook my head. Unruly children hurtled through the crowd, leaving staccato trails of curses and complaints in their wake. At small *warung* stalls, young men were selling banana fritters and 'shining mooncake' – two fat pancakes sandwiched together with jam.

Behind the plaza was a fruit and vegetable market. On parallel rows of covered tables, women from the villages sold mangoes, tomatoes, chillies, bananas and carrots, arranged into tidy piles. Those who could not afford to pay for the privilege of taking their place at the tables instead spread squares of sacking on the ground. Saumlaki housewives wandered from stall to stall, haggling over prices.

On either side of the vegetable market, buses sat with their engines idling. They belched thick exhaust clouds as they waited to fill with passengers. The buses were adorned with slogans in English: 'Cleanliness is Holiness', 'Love is Life'. Leaning out of the bus doors, wiry ticket collectors shouted their destinations over the hubbub of the crowd. When they were full, the vehicles lurched out of the marketplace to the villages beyond.

I stopped by a shop that sold pencils, pens, small snacks and tattered notebooks. The sign outside announced that this was a *toko buku*, a bookshop. Inside there was only a small shelf of books, mainly primers for schoolchildren on maths, Indonesian and English language. The shop owner lounged behind the counter, propped up by a photocopier. He was dressed in a string vest and sarong, and looked half asleep.

I said hello, and browsed through the books. At the end of the shelf was a small, slim volume with an orange cover. I pulled it off the shelf. On the cover was a line drawing of a cockatoo. The title, *Nangin Tanemprar*, was in the local language, Yamdenan. Underneath was written, in Indonesian, 'Folk Tales from Tanimbar'.

The book contained five stories in all, translated into Indonesian from the original Yamdenan and published by the missionary group the Summer Institute of Linguistics. There was no price on the cover. I asked the shop owner how much it was. He waved his hand and plucked a figure out of the air. It was cheap, so I bought it.

'You can read Indonesian?' the shopkeeper asked.

'With a dictionary,' I said.

He smiled. 'Well,' he said, 'this is a good book, a history book.'

'It says they are folk tales,' I said.

'Yes, folk tales. This is our history in Tanimbar. This is our *adat*.'

'Oh,' I said, looking down at the book.

'You will find it interesting,' the bookshop owner said, as he counted out my change.

That evening I sat on the pontoon looking out to sea. There was still a glimmer of evening sunlight coming from the west, turning the sea to fire. The water out in the bay was flat and calm. Frigate birds wheeled overhead. Sea eagles dived for fish. They plucked them, squirming, from the water and flew off to devour them. Across the other side of the bay, from behind the low line of trees, a thin tendril of smoke reached up to touch the thread-like clouds. It was the burning season, when the Tanimbarese 'clean the earth' – *cuci tanah* – preparing their plantations for sowing the new crop. It was beautiful, and yet I felt ill at ease. I thought of the hail of stones that had greeted my first appearance in the streets of Saumlaki. I thought of the Javanese businessman and his talk of *barang aneh* and strange phenomena. And I wondered what kind of a place it was in which I now found myself.

I opened up my copy of *Nangin Tanemprar* and, with the help of a dictionary, set about translating it into English. It was slow work, but it was absorbing and the attention that it required drove out my disquiet. Overhead the sky darkened, turning deep blue and then blackening to a beautiful, cloudless night. The Milky Way sprawled overhead, and the Southern Cross hung low in the sky. As the land cooled, a gentle breeze came in off the sea. Out in the bay the solitary lights of fishermen, night fishing with gas lamps, were reflected in the water. A man in some kind of uniform – a senior police official, it later turned out – came to sit outside with his subordinate by his side. He glumly ordered a beer for himself, but not for his sidekick. A little later a group of young, excitable Indonesian men appeared. They crowded round a large table beneath a weak light bulb, poring over plans and blueprints. They were engineers from Ambon, working on a road-building project. In a corner sat a plump, miserable woman drinking coffee alone. I learned later that she was from the island of Sumbawa. Her husband was working on a Taiwanese fishing boat moored in Tanimbarese waters. They were only recently married, and already her spouse was off at sea on a trawler. She spent most of her time sitting in the hotel, eating to ease her misery.

I ordered a beer. Then I took out my pen and started to translate the first tale in the book.

'*Nangin, nangin, O!*' the story began. 'A story, a story, Oh!'

Nangin, nangin, O!

There was husband and a wife. They had been married for four years, but had not yet had a child, so they lived in unhappiness. One day they went to the plantation to work. The husband told his wife he needed to go into the forest to cut a new ridgepole for the house. He went into the forest and left his wife alone.

When he had gone, his wife went to relieve herself. She found a secluded spot in which to squat. From her shit she made a ball, and out of this she fashioned a baby, moulding it carefully so it could become human. When she had finished her work, she saw that it was truly a child. She took it up in her arms and awaited the return of her husband.

When her husband returned, he was astonished. 'Where did you get that baby?' he asked.

'I bought it,' his wife answered. So the man lifted his new child into his arms and the three of them returned home to the village.

When the child was two months old, the parents went once more into the plantation to cut grass. As the baby was still young, the mother left it in the care of an old lady of the village. 'My husband and I are going into the plantation to cut grass,' she said. 'We will be back later in the day. We are giving you our child to look after. But remember: if the child cries, do not bathe him.' So saying, they went into the forest.

No sooner had they left than the child began to bawl. The old woman could not stop its wailing. 'There can be no harm,' she said to herself, 'in giving him just a little wash, so that he will be able to sleep all the better. Then I will be able to put him to bed clean and happy.'

The old woman went to prepare a basin of water to wash the baby. She took the child up into her arms and poured the water over his head. As soon as the first drop touched the baby's skin, the child turned back into a pile of shit.

The smell was revolting.

The old woman dropped the baby and ran from the house, laughing and spitting, muttering to herself, 'This child must have come from shit!'

When the other women of the village heard this commotion, they too came out of their houses, and gathered around to see what all the fuss was about. The old lady told them what had happened, and they laughed until they almost split their sides.

By the time I came to the end of my translation, the pontoon was almost empty. The night chirred with the sound of insects. Occasionally, over the lapping of the waves, I could hear the cough or cry of a night bird. I sat there, woozy with tiredness and with beer, and thought about the baby who had come from shit. What had the shopkeeper said? These were not folk tales. This was a book of history.

The lights of the fishing boats winked in the darkness. I had the strange sensation that the logic of this place in which I now found myself was out of reach. I looked out to sea and felt myself becoming unmoored, unanchored, cut adrift from my former certainties.

I closed my eyes, listing across some dark ocean on who knows what currents, whilst overhead there hung a cross fashioned out of stars.

Nangin, nangin, O!

A story, a story, Oh!

3

OUTSIDERS

I eased myself into life in Tanimbar by translating the tales from *Nangin Tanemprar*. Between bouts of translation, I wandered the town, trying to find people to talk to. Anthropology is a curious business. Insofar as it involves a method at all, the method, more or less, is this: you turn up somewhere, hang out, chat and write things down. The anthropologists somewhat grandly call this 'participant observation'. It is a surprisingly hard trick to pull off. Not only do you have to find the right people to hang out with, and not only do they have to put up with you, but it turns out that participation and observation aren't really compatible. They pull in opposite directions. When you find yourself participating fully, you forget to observe. When you observe, whipping out your notebook or tape recorder, you are withdrawing from participation.

One of my most pressing problems, early on, was finding people to talk to. Ideally, I wanted people who could unlock the secrets of the world I had just entered. I needed reliable informants, as anthropologists liked to call them. But these were the early days, and so I was willing to settle for anyone, however unreliable they might be. Conversation staves off the loneliness. It makes you feel as if you are serving some purpose. So in the first few days I wandered through Saumlaki and if somebody called out to me in the street, and if they seemed friendly, I went over to talk. Some were cranks. Some were curious. And some, over the months that followed, became good friends. The strategy worked. Soon I started to feel more at home in Tanimbar. Saumlaki was a small town, and after a few days I couldn't walk down the main street without meeting some acquaintance or other.

One afternoon, several days after my arrival, I found myself sitting on a bamboo bench in the village of Olilit Baru, a suburb of Saumlaki, with a group of men. There were five or six of them, mostly in middle age. It was early afternoon, and the sun was becoming hot. They had called me over to talk, and we were chatting about *adat*, so I decided to ask them about the shit-baby. They did not know the story, so I repeated it as best I could, in broken Indonesian. They listened attentively. At the end, all of the men nodded. I had expected them to laugh, but they looked serious. Yes, they said, this was the kind of thing that happened in Tanimbar.

A severe-looking man in his mid-forties spoke up. 'Let me give you another example,' he said. 'Have you got a notebook?' I had the sense that he had come across anthropologists before.

'Yes,' I said, reaching into my bag and pulling out my notebook. It was a large, green book with carbon paper that could be inserted between the pages, so that I could take copies of my notes. Every other page was perforated so it could be torn out.

'Write this down,' he said. 'There was a woman in my village who got pregnant. Sometime later she gave birth to an octopus.'

I scribbled notes, checking occasionally that I had understood. *An octopus?* Yes, an octopus. *With eight legs?* Yes, that's right.

'After the birth,' he went on, 'the mother took her baby to the best doctors in Ambon. They all confirmed it was an octopus. They proved it with science.'

'What happened to the child?' I asked.

'The mother came home and threw it into the sea,' the man said, as if my question was so obvious it did not need to be asked at all. Then he leaned towards me. 'But every full moon night, the woman goes to the shore and meets with her son. They embrace for a while, and then her child returns to the deepest part of the sea. It has to live in the deep sea, so it does not get caught by fishermen.'

'Do you know the family?' I asked.

'Of course,' he said. 'And I have proof that the story is true.'

I hesitated, my pen hovering over the page. 'Proof?' I asked.

'The family do not eat octopus any more,' he said, 'in case they eat their own child.'

My pen continued to hover.

'You don't believe me,' he said.

'No,' I said. 'I don't.'

He frowned. 'You foreigners from England and America, you never believe these things. But you will see.' Then, for some reason, he started to laugh. He laughed so much, I found myself joining in, and all the other men started laughing as well. But after a moment, my informant became serious. 'This is not a joke,' he said. 'I cannot make you believe. You people think you know everything with your science. But you do not know Tanimbar. This is how things happen here. We are the people who live here. We see these *barang aneh* with our own eyes.'

𖤓

Several days later, I met Pastor Böhm, the Tanimbar Islands' last Dutch missionary. All Western visitors to Tanimbar, if they stayed long enough, ended up having an audience with Pastor Böhm. The priest had come to the Tanimbar Islands in the mid-1960s and had been there ever since. He lived on the outskirts of Saumlaki in a small seminary complex owned by the Catholic church. I had been put in touch with him by an Australian friend who knew him well.

It was evening as I walked through the scrubby gardens of the *pastoran*. A group of young seminarians was playing volleyball on the dusty sports ground. Others sat in the dwindling light and looked on. Many young men entered the seminary to train for the priesthood, but not so many stayed the course. In a part of the world where educational opportunities were few, a seminary education gave many a head start.

I waved to the young seminarians. They called back in greeting. 'Hello, Mister! How are you?'

I knocked on the door of the *pastoran*. A thin, vigorous and rather short man opened the door. He was dressed in sandals, a short-sleeved batik shirt that was open at the neck and a pair of old, worn trousers. His expression was serious, although his mouth had a wry twist to it.

He smiled. 'Come in,' he said. His Dutch-inflected English sounded both courteous and strangely impatient. 'Please, sit down.'

He ushered me into the *pastoran*. I sat down at the table. 'Would you like a beer?' he asked.

'Yes, thanks.'

He went to collect two bottles of Anker beer and cracked them open, passing one in my direction. 'Right,' he said, holding up the bottle, 'let us begin.'

'Cheers!' I said.

'Cheers!' Pastor Böhm replied. He lifted his glass and drank, his Adam's apple bobbing up and down. He sighed with satisfaction as he returned the glass to the table. The cold beer was welcome after the heat of the day. Outside the door, a fat gecko was making a racket. In another building somewhere across the courtyard, the seminary choir started up. I could hear their enthusiastic singing, accompanied by an electronic keyboard. I could not catch the words, but the tunes were familiar. The gecko did its best to compete.

'So,' the priest said, 'what brings you to Tanimbar?'

✗

I warmed to the last Dutch missionary. He had a quick mind and an appetite for conversation. We finished our beers, and he replenished them. Outside, night fell quickly. We talked about life in Tanimbar. I told him about the shit-baby.

He laughed. 'Ah,' he said, 'these people – they believe all kinds of things without any evidence, you know?'

Momentarily, I wondered if babies made from shit, or women who gave birth to octopuses, were inherently more implausible than virgin births or resurrections from the dead. But Pastor Böhm was a man of pragmatic temperament. He was the kind of man who liked evidence, who would risk censure to poke his hands in the wounded side of a recently returned Messiah, just to make sure. I liked this about him. I liked the robust faith he had in reason and its fruits. And I liked the note of pride I detected in him when he talked about life on the Tanimbar Islands. Early on in his tenure, when the roads were less good, he told me, he went everywhere on foot, even to the most remote villages. He carried his luggage on his back, walking fast and chain-smoking as he went.

A friend later told me that as a young man he had accompanied the pastor on several of these missions. He had been incapable of keeping up. 'Pastor Böhm is very strong,' he said, shaking his head ruefully. 'He walks too fast. All that smoking makes him strong.'

When the beer ran out, Pastor Böhm sat back. It was getting late. 'Well,' he said, 'tomorrow I have an early start.'

I took this as my cue to leave, and started to make my excuses.

Pastor Böhm held up his hand. 'A couple of other things,' he said. 'If you get the chance, you should go to the school and talk to Suster Astrid. She is a nun, a good woman. She will help you out. Tell her that I sent you to speak with her. And before you go, let me give you something.'

He got up and went into the back room. He returned carrying a large yellow-bound book. 'This will keep you busy,' he said. 'The Indonesian is not beautiful, but if you can't read Dutch, it is the best that you have.'

The book was called *Etnografi Tanimbar,* the Indonesian translation of a Dutch ethnography of the Tanimbar Islands, *Het Leven van den Tanémbarees. Ethnographische studie over het Tanémbareesche volk,* written by the Catholic priest Petrus Drabbe, one of Pastor Böhm's predecessors. Drabbe had lived in Tanimbar for two decades between 1915 and 1935. After leaving Tanimbar, he moved to Merauke in Western New Guinea, and it was there that he wrote the book, drawing upon his comprehensive notes. The book was a masterpiece of painstaking thoroughness and insight. Had it originally been written in French or in English, rather than Dutch, it might have entered the canon of twentieth-century anthropological classics. As it was, it was little known outside of the Dutch-speaking world. The Indonesian translation had been made by Karel Mouw, an amateur Tanimbarese ethnographer from the island of Larat. It had been painstakingly typed out on a manual typewriter and xeroxed.

I put the copy of *Etnografi Tanimbar* under my arm and the priest led me to the door. I stepped into the night. There was a cool breeze coming off the sea. For a moment, Pastor Böhm hesitated on the threshold, looking thoughtful. Then he smiled.

'You know,' he said. 'I have been here for a very long time. I have seen many people pass through Tanimbar. They come here for many different reasons, but one thing is always true. If they want what they are looking for enough, they always find it.'

I smiled. 'Thanks,' I said. 'That's encouraging.'

'Good luck,' the priest said. 'Come and visit from time to time and tell me how you are getting on.'

As I walked back into town, I wondered what the pastor had been looking for when he came to Tanimbar. I wondered whether he had found it. Then I asked myself what it was that I was looking for. And I realised I was not entirely sure.

ᛉ

Sometime during my first week in Saumlaki, I met with the school-teacher Benny Fenyapwain. Benny was a former seminarian. He had left the training for the priesthood on account of his philosophical and doctrinal perplexities, and he now taught English in the school in Saumlaki. In his spare time, he collected recordings of old music from the villages. He had a keen interest in anthropology, a sharp mind and a delight in the absurdity of life. He soon became not just an informant (how cold that term sounded!), but also a friend.

Benny owned a motorbike, and he offered to take me on a tour to explore nearby villages. He picked me up at the Harapan Indah one morning, and we headed up the road to Olilit Tua.

'There is a monument I want you to see,' he said. 'You are interested in sculpture, so I think you will like it.'

We arrived in Olilit Tua and Benny and I dismounted. The monument turned out to be a diorama showing four scantily clad, dark-skinned Tanimbarese in attitudes of prayer. They knelt at the feet of a single solemn-looking white priest. Behind the priest's head the dove of the Holy Spirit cast its light.

The Catholic missions to Tanimbar arrived in 1910. The first two priests, Father Cappers and Father Klerks, brought with them all the home comforts they needed for a long-term stay: petrol, gunpowder, sleeping mats and pillows, as well as two catechists and two servants. They set about building makeshift schools in the villages of Olilit and Lauran. Soon after, a group of Protestant missionaries turned up. The Protestants brought with them a platoon of soldiers for protection, and began to set up a rival school. The Tanimbarese, however, did not appreciate the presence of armed strangers in their midst. They took up arms against the Protestants. In response, the Dutch authorities in Ambon launched a punitive force of forty infantrymen, under the command of Lieutenant van den Bossche. The Lieutenant sailed to Tanimbar and slaughtered dozens of people. Then he deported seventy local leaders to

Ambon in chains. An uneasy peace ensued as Tanimbar now came, for the first time, under Dutch colonial rule. The Dutch banned headhunting and dancing, the use of lime to bleach men's hair, and any extended public celebrations that might occasion 'lewdness' and 'immorality'.

None of this, of course, did anything for the reputation of the Protestant missionaries. Hearts and minds are not won through the barrel of a gun. The Catholics distanced themselves from these brutal wranglings, and came out of the whole business pretty well. Meanwhile, the Protestants laid the blame at the door of Father Klerks and his Catholic followers, claiming it was they who had incited the local population to violence. The Dutch colonial powers took the accusation seriously enough to summon Klerks to Ambon to explain himself. But the Catholics were cleared of all charges. In the calm that followed this most bloody of beginnings, the Catholic priests set about converting the local population. Meanwhile, the Protestants slunk away to try their luck instead in the northern parts of the Tanimbar Islands. The monument in Olilit Tua marked the spot of the first Catholic baptisms, which took place two years later.

The text on the monument read:

MEMORIAL MONUMENT
Receiving the Sacrament of the First Baptism
by:
Pastor L. Niemenhuis, MSc, on the date of the 3rd April 1913
Pastor Yoseph Klerks, MSc, on the date of the 24th July 1913
Pastor Eduard Cappers MSc, on the date of the 24th July 1913
in Olilit
A Milestone in the History
of the Development of the Catholic Religion
in Tanimbar

There was something unsettling about the kneeling, half-naked figures of the Tanimbarese and the pale-skinned, fully dressed priest.

'I know the sculptor,' Benny said. 'He makes sculptures from concrete. His only tool is a flattened spoon.'

'A spoon?'

Benny grinned. 'A spoon,' he said.

Before the arrival of Cappers and Klerks, before the Dutch punitive raids, Tanimbar had been a fiercely independent place. But Cappers and Klerks were by no means the first outsiders to come to the islands. For centuries the Tanimbarese had traded with Buginese and Arab merchants, and the islands were known in the West at least since Mercator's nautical map of 1569. The Dutch first visited in 1636, building a fort on the northern island of Fordata, from where they traded in slaves, tortoiseshells and shark fins. However, compared with the riches of the Spice Islands to the north, Tanimbar had little to offer the European powers. By the next century the fort had fallen into ruin and the Dutch had departed.

In the nineteenth century, interest in Tanimbar was rekindled by the European colonialists' mania for filling in the holes in the map. In 1822, a schooner called the *Stedcombe* set sail from London. On board was Joseph Forbes, the son of a shoemaker. When the schooner moored off the shore of Yamdena two years later, there was an altercation with the locals and Forbes was taken captive. 'Timor Joe', as he later became known, was held as a slave for the next fifteen years. In the account he dictated later, he claimed he was 'kept by the natives to hard labour such as cutting Timber, cultivating yams, Plantains, Sweet Potatoes, etc which from the oppressive heat of the climate has ruined my constitution'. He was rescued in 1839 by the British vessel, the *Essington*. Thomas Watson, captain of the *Essington*, found Forbes in poor shape. The captive was confused, speaking only the most rudimentary and broken English, his body covered in burns and ulcerated sores. 'Nor does the Catalogue of this poor fellow's misfortunes end here,' Watson wrote in his log, 'for he was found to have been injured in the Genitals, and on being questioned about it, he said it was caused by the bite of the Native Wild Pig.' Forbes returned to London, but was restless and incapable of settling. He boarded another ship and eventually ended up in Williamstown, Australia, where he is buried.

Forbes was perhaps the first British visitor to Tanimbar, but he was not the last. As the century wore on, Tanimbar became increasingly subject to often-unwelcome attention from outsiders. In 1882, the Scottish naturalist Henry Ogg Forbes – no relation to the unfortunate Timor Joe – arrived with his recently wed wife, Anna. Both Henry and Anna left valuable accounts of the warlike, headhunting Tanimbarese. But Henry also decided to take advantage of his presence in Tanimbar to embark upon a little headhunting of his own. In keeping with the anthropological mania of the times, whilst in Tanimbar he accumulated a number of local skulls for the purposes of scientific study. Henry was puzzled by the Tanimbarese response to his collecting. He wrote:

> It seems as if there existed in these countries a superstitious dread of any part of their person being in possession of another. One day, when I purchased from a man his father's skull, something of the same dread appeared; for as soon as the bargain was completed, the seller took from his *luvu* (or *siri*-holder) a piece of areca-nut, and, setting the skull before him, he placed the nut between its teeth, and before handing it over to me he repeated a long and devout invocation.

It is as if, had a Tanimbarese traveller turned up in a village in Stirlingshire or Wiltshire and calmly asked for the head of the host's deceased father, this might be greeted with calm and unruffled equanimity.

Tanimbar's relationship with outsiders, then, had never been straightforward, and was marked by violence and brutality on all sides. But in the end it was the outsiders who prevailed. By the time the Catholic priest Petrus Drabbe arrived in 1915, the days of Tanimbar's independence were numbered. Part way through his stay in the islands, the priest wrote a melancholic letter home, setting out his qualms about the mission of which he was a part. 'More than I care for, and more than is good,' he wrote, 'people are gradually throwing everything away, that which is from their ancestors and authentically Tanimbarese.'

I took a few photographs of the monument, then Benny and I walked down to the beach and looked out to sea. I didn't say anything for a long time. The sculpture was troubling me. On the surface, it seemed a simple story: since the nineteenth century, the Tanimbarese had given up their independence; they had knelt before the outsiders – the Dutch, the Japanese, the champions of the Indonesian state – and bowed their heads in submission. But I felt myself implicated in all this. Wasn't I just the latest in a long line of outsiders? And as I mistrusted all the others, so I mistrusted myself.

Yet it occurred to me that, for all this, Drabbe was wrong. There was something stubbornly, persistently Tanimbarese that had not yet been overcome by all these external forces.

I turned to Benny. 'Have you heard the story about the woman who gave birth to an octopus?' I asked him.

He laughed. 'An octopus?' he asked. 'No.'

'I was told it by a man I met in Olilit Baru,' I said. Then I told Benny the story.

When the story was done, he grinned and shrugged. 'People here believe in strange things,' he said.

We left the priest and his converts alone, climbed onto the motorbike and puttered back into Saumlaki.

PART II

JAMAN PURBA

THE ANCIENT AGE

Matias Fatruan, from Rumah Salut, Sera

4

BEGINNINGS

There is no one way of telling a history. Or perhaps there is no single history to be told. Babies coming from shit, women giving birth to octopuses. *This is our history*, the man in the bookshop told me. That night, as I sat in the Harapan Indah drinking beer, I traced the threads of these stories back to their very beginnings. I traced them back to long before the anthropologists and the missionaries came. To long before Henry Ogg Forbes' headhunting expeditions and Joseph Forbes' extended captivity. To long before the maps of Tanimbar were drawn up. To before the archipelago took shape and form. At that time – *in illo tempore*, as the great scholar of myth and religion Mircea Eliade was fond of saying – in the time of origins, there was a hero. And the hero's name was Atuf.

Drabbe salvaged the stories of Atuf just as they were on the brink of being told no more. Today, they are remembered and retold because of him. They have a new life, even if it is not quite the life they had before. Under the Southern Cross, I worked through the Indonesian translation of the Dutch priest's book. Those stories that had been told in Yamdenan and Fordatan, translated into Dutch and then rendered in Indonesian – I clumsily translated them a further time into English. And still the figure of Atuf remained, compelling and strange, through all these iterations and reiterations.

It was with Atuf that everything began.

It was Atuf who set time in motion.

It was Atuf who severed land from sea and earth from sky, male from female and the sun from the moon.

It was Atuf who birthed the scatter of stars suspended over my head.

Atuf was a nobleman from the island of Babar, eighty miles to the west of Tanimbar. He lived in luxury with his sisters Inkelu, Yaum Aratwenan and Mangmwatabun.

'Atuf's family were high nobles,' Drabbe wrote. 'They were so high that they didn't work, didn't labour in the gardens, didn't fetch and carry water or anything like that.'

But the people of Babar become impatient with these idle overlords. They rose up to drive Atuf and his sisters out of Babar for good. The siblings took a war canoe, and a magic spear that had been wrested from the drunkard god Ubila'a. They headed east over the choppy seas to Tanimbar, a gloomy place where land and sea, earth and sky, male and female had yet to be split apart.

There was something strange about Inkelu and her sisters. They were mixed by nature, intersex. As one man from the village of Sifnana told the American anthropologist Susan McKinnon, Inkelu and her sisters were 'half woman, half man'. Inkelu, in particular, was a drinker of *sopi* – palm-wine, traditionally a male drink. She was a hunter and a warrior, and wore a sarong, making it impossible to see what lay beneath. Later, Inkelu was to die in battle, beheaded, having massacred countless enemies.

The sisters settled in different places: Inkelu on the island of Asutubun, or Dog Cape, close to Olilit; Mangmwatabun on the island of Selaru; Yaum Aratwenan heading north to Omtufu. As for Atuf, he made his home in the village of Sifnana. But he was dissatisfied with his new home. The sun brooded, a heavy red abscess on the horizon. Sometimes it rose a little, but then it sank back under the burden of its own weight. The sky was low – stifling and oppressive. So Atuf took up his spear and began to slice islands from the mainland, opening up channels so that fresh rivers could flow in Tanimbar, shaping land and sea, carving a new world.

Atuf was the first sculptor, fashioning the raw material that was Tanimbar. It was Atuf who gave shape to the undifferentiated mass of land and sea. When he was done with his carving, he summoned some slaves and they prepared their war canoe to sail for the eastern horizon. Before he left, Atuf danced in the prow of the boat. His sister Inkelu, seeing his dance was clumsy and heavy-footed, came to join him and taught him how to dance the way the frigate birds soared above, dipping and stooping and swaying, the way women still dance in Tanimbar. And as Inkelu demonstrated this dance to Atuf, he joined in. He cast off his inelegance and clumsiness, and the two of them danced together – a sister who was half male and half female, a brother dancing a woman's dance – celebrating their final moments together.

When the dancing was done, Atuf and his slaves cast off from the shore. Stowed in the bottom of the canoe were clamshells filled with coconut milk. As the party sailed closer to the sun and the heat became more intense, they bathed their bodies in the cooling milk. The nearer they came to the horizon, the lower the sky hung over their heads. They sliced off the top of the mast to avoid becoming stuck between the sky and the sea. As they drew closer to the sun, the sea boiled angrily about them. The boards of the canoe smoked and blackened. Then Atuf raised a wooden plank to shelter himself from the heat, took aim with the magic spear and thrust it into the heart of the furnace.

The sun shattered into a million parts. A large piece came free and fell into the sea. It hissed and spluttered and let up a plume of steam. When it rose the following night, cool and white, it was a new moon. Countless fragments were scattered across the sky, and these became the stars. Dripping the red blood of dawn, the sun rose and cast light over the Tanimbar Islands for the first time. Thus was time set in motion.

Atuf did not live long to enjoy the fruits of his heroism. As the victorious party sailed back home, they stopped off near the cape of Lamdesar in the northern part of the archipelago, on an island where the mango trees grew upside down, dropping their fruits upward into the sky. Atuf went ashore. He asked his slaves to wait, then he squatted down. Even heroes need to shit. As he shat, Atuf found himself becoming stuck fast to the ground, and turned to stone. Perhaps he should have taken his cue from the mango trees, and shat whilst standing on his head. Perhaps then the story would have been different.

It is said that you can see him even now, if you look carefully enough – though the mango trees have long gone – a squatting figure fixed in stone, just off the cape of Lamdesar, emptying his bowels for all eternity.

The slaves returned home without Atuf. When they stepped ashore, they turned instantly into tree shrews. They scuttled into the forest, and were gone.

Ж

Several days later, Benny said he would take me to meet Suster Astrid. 'You will like her,' he said. 'She will help you. We can go and visit her in the school tomorrow morning.'

The next day, I was up early. I breakfasted on pancakes and coffee sweetened with condensed milk on the pontoon at the back of the Harapan Indah. As I ate, I worked my way through Drabbe's ethnography. Benny turned up some time around eight thirty, and we walked up to the school together. When we arrived, the pupils were standing to attention as the Indonesian red and white flag – the *merah-putih* – was hoisted in the school courtyard. The nun, a reassuringly friendly woman in starched white, nodded at me in greeting and gave me a grin of breathtaking loveliness. Then she held up a hand to tell me to wait. The schoolkids nudged each other and giggled to see an *orang bule*, a

Westerner, standing there in their schoolyard. Suster Astrid shushed them as they saluted and sang.

Indonesia, tanah airku
Tanah tumpah darahku
Di sanalah aku berdiri
Jadi pandu ibuku

Indonesia, my homeland
The land of my spilled blood
Here I stand, to become
The vanguard of my motherland

Once the song was done, the pupils filed off to their classes. Some of the braver ones waved at me and called out 'Hello, Mister!'

Suster Astrid came over to shake my hand. 'William,' she said, 'Pastor Böhm told me about you. Welcome to our school. How are you liking Tanimbar? Would you like tea?'

'Yes, thank you,' I said.

Suster Astrid introduced me to her colleague, a serious and practical-looking woman called Ibu Neli. Together they took us into the kitchen where we drank sugary tea and talked. Ibu Neli passed around a plate of sago biscuits. Suster Astrid was extraordinarily animated. As she talked, she joked, broke into song, slapped her thighs, laughed heartily, pulled faces and teased Ibu Neli for her seriousness. The nun had been in Tanimbar since just after her ordination and now she divided her time between the school and the small under-equipped clinic in the town – 'helping people', as she put it, with the most exquisite smile. And because she had been a long time in Tanimbar, and had helped so very many people, it turned out that Suster Astrid was extremely well connected.

We talked about my plans for the coming months. Suster Astrid told me there was a sculptor on the island of Sera to the west. His name was Matias and he made sculptures for the church, but he also made more traditional work.

'I think you should go there,' she said.

At this point, Ibu Neli broke in. There had recently been a church festival, she said. Her relatives from Sera, Ibu and Bapak Malinda, were in Saumlaki. They were heading back to Sera by boat in the next couple of days, and I might be able to catch a lift with them. Ibu Neli said she would speak with them.

'I will ask them if you can go with them. Sera is not an easy place to be,' she said. 'You will be safe with them.'

'Not easy,' Suster Astrid said, 'but interesting.' She beamed again.

I left the school mid-morning and headed back into town. I walked through the Yamdena Plaza down to the harbour and along the concrete jetty that jutted out into the bay, where the trading boats and small craft were moored. There were some kids fooling around on the deck of one of the boats, jumping off the side into the cool water. I sat down at the end of the jetty, and looked into the water, watching the crabs go to and fro amongst the rubble as they foraged for carrion. The day was becoming hot and the air beginning to shimmer. I breathed in the sea air. I was getting used to Tanimbar; I was beginning to like it. I looked out over the bay. It was a beautiful day. The kids shouted out 'Hello, Mister!' and the frigate birds wheeled overhead, like Inkelu and Atuf dancing on the deck of their war canoe. I took out my notebook and scribbled a few notes. Then I closed it again, and just sat, looking across the water, feeling the sun warm my skin.

Bapak Malinda turned up at the Harapan Indah that afternoon. He was a serious, unsmiling man, with a slight build, a dark complexion and blood-shot eyes. He said I would be welcome to stay with them as a guest in Sera, but warned me, as had Suster Astrid, that Sera was a hard place to live.

'If you wish to come to Sera, you must be our guest,' he said, 'but our house is very simple. You will not be comfortable there. It will be difficult for you.'

I reassured him that I would be delighted to stay. He seemed hesitant and nervous. He stood in front of me, shuffling his feet.

'Sera is a bad place,' he said. 'The people in Sera are bad people. They are coarse and dishonest.' Then he added, as if this was sufficient explanation for this coarseness and dishonesty, 'They are *Protestants*.'

I reassured him that I was not afraid of Protestants.

'Then, if you want to come,' he said, smiling shyly, 'make sure that you are ready tomorrow morning at seven thirty. We will come and collect you and take you to the docks.'

I got up at six the following morning, and packed a small bag. I stowed most of my books and other possessions in a store cupboard in the Harapan Indah hotel. After breakfast, I waited in the foyer for Bapak Malinda's arrival.

By nine o'clock he still had not arrived, so I walked down to the docks to see what was happening. I asked around, but there were no boats going to Sera. I returned to the Harapan Indah, and continued to wait. Close to ten o'clock, when I had all but given up, Bapak Malinda came hurtling in from the street, wild eyed and anxious.

'William! We are late!' he cried. 'The minibus is waiting!'

He tugged me out into the street. Outside was a minibus with its engine running. The roof was laden with sacks of provisions – rice and dried fish and other goods cheaper in Saumlaki than in Sera. Anxious faces pressed up against the window. Bapak Malinda ushered me into the bus. He climbed in beside me. On my other side his wife, Ibu Malinda, introduced herself with a thin smile. It was cramped in the back of the minibus. I hunched over my bag and smiled at the other passengers. The bus pulled away from the hotel. It careered down to the far end of the jetty where it stopped, and we all clambered out.

Then the hurry was over. The boat was there, bobbing against the hanging rows of tyres at the side of the jetty. It was a small, dumpy craft, the boards of its deck aged and weathered. There was a single engine at the rear, and a wooden porch sheltered the deck from the rain and the sun. On board were fifteen or twenty passengers, dozing and wrapped in sarongs. Bapak Malinda seemed to relax to see that the boat had not already left. He climbed up on top of the minibus and untied the sacks. I tried to help lift them to the ground, but Bapak Malinda told me to stop. I was his guest, he said. Guests should not move sacks of dried fish. I should get on the boat and rest.

I boarded the boat and watched as the luggage was loaded on board. The other passengers eyed me with lukewarm curiosity. The engine was already running, the deck vibrating. The throb of the engine made me feel sleepy. I leaned against the side of the porch and closed my eyes. I was not sure what to expect of Sera; I had become accustomed to Saumlaki, I had started to make friends. And now here I was again, in the company of almost-total strangers, about to put to sea in search of an island about which I knew almost nothing other than its name.

Once everything was loaded, Bapak and Ibu Malinda came to join me. It was the first time we had a chance to properly introduce ourselves. Bapak and Ibu Malinda said they were schoolteachers. They had been posted to the island shortly after their marriage. They hadn't particularly wanted to marry each other, Bapak Malinda told me with astonishing frankness, but their families had insisted. His wife nodded, as if this was just a fact of life.

'These things are burdens,' they said. 'We do them out of duty.'

I realised that I, too, was simply another burden within a life that was nothing more than a series of burdens, one more duty to shoulder.

I had presumed that departure was imminent. But it was another four hours before we eventually chugged out of Saumlaki. Bapak and Ibu Malinda disappeared into town on some last-minute mission. I sat looking out to sea as we bobbed on the tide in silence. Nobody spoke much. The passengers just sat and watched the waves and the people coming and going on the jetty.

Bapak and Ibu Malinda returned with some *ketupat* – rice parcels wrapped inside woven palm leaves – and some cold grilled fish. They passed me the rice and fish, and I ate.

Towards afternoon, the boat cast off. When we came out of the sheltering bay, the sea was surprisingly choppy. Despite the bright sunshine, the breeze made the air cold. The island of Selaru was to the south, and to the west were the sparkling waters of the open sea. Somewhere over the horizon, I knew, was Babar, the ancestral home of Atuf.

We headed west around the foot of Yamdena. The sun was beginning to sink in the western sky. The boat rose and fell on the swell. A little later, we turned northwards, following the western coast of Yamdena. My fellow passengers became more garrulous. Where was I from? What was I doing in Tanimbar? Why was I going to Sera? Did I miss my mother? Was I married? What did I think about Indonesian women?

Then a thin, serious-looking, elderly man spoke. He introduced himself as the headman of one of the five villages on the north coast of Sera. He wore the thick-rimmed glasses of a scholar, and had a thoughtful air. He started to talk, for no reason in particular, about the Second World War, and about the Japanese occupation of Tanimbar.

'It was terrible,' he told me. 'In my village they threw a man into a pit full of bamboo spikes. They beat him from above with sticks until he bled to death. We were afraid of the Japanese. We hid out in the forest with the ghosts and spirits. We were afraid of ghosts and spirits, but we were more afraid of the Japanese, so we went into the forest to hide. But things are better now. Now we are at peace. Now we are free within Indonesia.' He pointed to our starboard side. 'The village there,' he said, pointing to where the surf was breaking on the reef, 'is Latdalam.' Then he pointed up the coast. 'Further up there you fill find Makatian. It is the oldest village in Tanimbar. There are many *barang aneh* in Makatian, many strange things.'

'For example?' I asked.

'They say that in the forest outside the village there are five chests of gold, brought by the English.'

'The English?' I said. 'When did they bring the gold?'

He thought for a while. 'Hundreds,' he said, 'perhaps thousands of years ago. It is still there, out in the forest.'

'Nobody has stolen it?'

The headman frowned. 'Nobody would dare. They are all too frightened. It is protected by magic.' Then he added, on a more practical note, 'Besides, nobody can remember where it is.'

Next, a large woman, who had been sitting silently towards the stern, spoke up. 'That is not all,' she said, as if to better the headman's story. 'There is a stone statue in the woods outside the village of Makatian that was made in America hundreds of years ago. It is very sacred.'

The headman, not to be outdone, spoke again. 'You see, *Tuan*, there are many wonderful things in Makatian. There is the tusk of a pig two feet in length. It was a giant pig that was once human. It happened like this: there was a man who was dancing, and as he danced, he was struck by an arrow and turned into a pig. Then he died. They took one of his tusks and ground it up. The powdered tusk rubbed onto the shaft of an arrow ensures that the shot is true. The other tusk is still in the village. You can still see it today. All this is in Makatian.'

Fragments of things I had read about the Tanimbar Islands started to come back to me: the connections that were drawn between pigs, hunting and death; how the souls of the sick appeared in the forest as pigs, where they were stumbled upon by hunters. If the hunter shot the pig, the patient would die. If the hunter missed, the patient would live. Then I remembered the Tanimbarese man I met in Holland who told me a strange tale about the uncanny American anthropologist who wandered in the forests and talked with the spirits. I told the headman about this.

'Yes,' he said, 'I have heard these tales.'

Sera appeared to our port side, low lying and forested. The sun was touching the sea now. On deck it was becoming cold. The captain of the boat shouted at us, and gesticulated towards the bows of the boat, distracting us from our storytelling. We were moving into the shallows, and the captain was eager to make sure we did not run aground. We clustered around the sides of the boat, on the lookout for sandbanks. The corridor between Sera to our port side and Yamdena to the starboard side was narrow. We puttered through slowly, without becoming stuck fast.

When we had cleared the shallows, we turned west into the setting sun. The headman resumed his storytelling. He pointed to a large, low-lying island to the north.

'Selu,' he said.

'Selu,' I repeated.

'The island of the dead,' said the headman.

Bapak Malinda leaned towards me. 'Selu is a dangerous place,' he whispered. 'There is nobody living on the island, but by night you can see the lights carried by the dead as they walk the cape. When we see these things, we are afraid.'

The anthropologist Nico de Jonge writes of how in Maluku it is believed that after death a person's 'shadow image' lives on. Several days after death, this shadow takes up a new home in a village of the dead, 'usually situated on an uninhabited island, a reef or a cape, not far from the world of the living'. I looked towards the north. I could see no lights in the dusk, but there was a boat moored close to the shore.

'What is that boat doing?' I asked.

'Fishermen from Taiwan,' said Bapak Malinda.

'Isn't it dangerous for them also?' I asked.

'Yes it is, but they do not know. They are foreigners, so they do not know. But people must not go to Selu. If they do, and if they walk in the forest, they fall asleep by the power of magic, and then they wake up in the middle of the sea where they drown. This has happened to many people. This is our *adat*.'

The sky was darkening over Sera. The thick mangrove swamps to the south gave way to beaches. Beyond the beaches, pinprick lights of paraffin lamps burned, strung out in a line along the north coast. The dark drew in. The garrulous passengers continued to trade tales with the whispered hush and shudder that has, since the beginning of time, accompanied night-time stories of the uncanny. The shivers that ran down my spine were not only on account of the sea breeze. I did not believe the tales I was hearing. But I could not dismiss them entirely. They were so firmly rooted in the landscape, in the shallow seas and tiny villages that clung tenaciously to the low rocks, in the twisted roots of the mangrove swamps and the low, scrubby forests, that it was impossible to reject their strange undertow. The stories belonged to the landscape, and the landscape to the stories. And, because I was a part of that landscape, they seeped into me, whether I liked it or not. I felt the strange logic of Tanimbarese myth and story beginning to work on me. It was a logic rooted in concrete things, in rocks and stones and cliffs that plunged down to the sea. To spend time in a place is to become subject to its logic, whether one likes it or not. Perhaps this was why anthropologists, on returning from the field, often retain a certain wild-eyed strangeness. Redomesticated, they settle into their university offices. They mark essay scripts, meet with students, write sober research papers for learned journals, drink mugs of coffee. But they remain strange, because part of them has been subjected to elsewhere; part of them belongs to elsewhere.

As we chugged slowly across the surface of the dark sea, the village lights wavering in the dark, the waves lapping against the bows of the boat, I shuddered again. I told myself I was being irrational. There were no capes where the dead walked. But there is nothing less rational than the notion that we can or should be entirely rational beings. In a place such as this, who was to say that a baby could not be born from shit? Who was to say that a woman could not transform into a pig? Who was to say that there were not cliffs and promontories upon which the dead walked with their lights at night?

We weighed anchor some way out from the shore. Everyone fell silent. In the sky was a cold moon. I looked towards the shore.

5

ANTHROPOLOGISTS AND THIEVES

A fleet of dugout canoes came out to meet us. Bapak Malinda disembarked before me, so he could give prior warning to his family of my coming. They would not be expecting me: there were no telephones on Sera. He asked me to wait on board until he returned.

Several passengers clambered into the dugouts and were gone. Soon, Bapak Malinda reappeared, paddling his own canoe. I clambered down from the little motorboat. It was a delicate procedure. I teetered inelegantly as I shuffled up towards the stern. Several passengers clambered down onto Bapak Malinda's canoe behind me. They loaded sacks of produce on board. When there were seven of us in all, balanced either in the body of the boat or leaning out on the wooden outriggers, Bapak Malinda began to row with swift, strong strokes of the paddle. The sides of the dugout were low in the water, barely more than a couple of inches above the surface. The water was black, except where it reflected the broken moonlight.

When we were close to the shore, Bapak Malinda let the canoe drift. He jumped out into the water, and nodded to me that I should do the same. It was only a couple of feet deep and the water was warmer than the chill of the night air. Bapak Malinda pulled the canoe to its moorings. Unloading the sacks of rice bought in Saumlaki, we waded ashore through the dark. Everybody was tired from the journey. Nobody objected when I helped unload the baggage.

On the beach was Bapak Malinda's teenage daughter, waiting with a paraffin lamp. She smiled and introduced herself, shaking my hand.

'You should go with her,' Bapak Malinda said. Then he climbed back into the canoe and headed back towards the motorboat to pick up a few more passengers.

Bapak Malinda's daughter led me up a back lane to the house, stopping me at the door and holding her lamp so that the light fell on my feet. They were covered in mud. She gave me a bucket of water, and stood over me as I washed off the mud, making sure I did the job properly. Then she smiled and invited me in. The rest of the family emerged from the back of the house. We sat down on hard wooden chairs. Neighbours, curious to see this new guest, crowded into the room. Bapak Malinda's daughter disappeared into the kitchen. She returned soon after with a tray on which were several glasses of tea. I was tired from the journey, and from a long day of speaking Indonesian, but I did my best to play the good guest as I ate dry, salty biscuits and drank tea.

When I had finished, Bapak Malinda ushered the onlookers out. His wife put a bed in the corner of the room, and cordoned it off with a makeshift curtain.

'You can sleep here,' she said. 'I hope you will be comfortable.'

For the rest of the evening we talked and ate. My Indonesian had noticeably improved over the previous few weeks, but I was exhausted, and it was a relief when Ibu Malinda suggested I go to bed. I wished everyone good night and disappeared behind the curtain. The family and their visitors slowly dispersed.

I tried to sleep, but I was restless. Outside in the street, the village dogs were howling. Whenever my mind drifted, I found it churning with strange, unsettling images: women who turned into pigs, capes where the dead walked at night, gold hidden in the forest. I turned over again and again. The bed was uncomfortable. There was rustling in the rafters. And beyond the throb of insect life and the howl of the dogs, there was a silence deeper than any I was used to. I began to slip into confused dreams, then lurched awake, then drifted away again.

I woke not long after dawn, the village cockerels putting up a racket. On the other side of the curtain, I could hear the swish of a brush as the Malindas' daughter swept the room clean. I lay for as long as I thought I could get away with, relishing the solitude. I knew that once I emerged, I would have no more time to myself. I would have to talk, and talk some more, and talk even more.

The one thing that I had not fully anticipated about fieldwork was the sheer strain of having to interact hour after hour and day after day. I had not expected how much effort it would take to get out of bed and make new acquaintances. This was only compounded by the difficulty of wrestling constantly with a language I only spoke badly, and by the painful, stuttering process of working out what the hell was going on around me. I had a sense that the Malinda family – these good, kind people who had invited me into their home, and who I knew would look after me as long as I wished to stay – already found my presence a burden and a weight. I wondered by what right I was there, in this small village, imposing myself on these strangers. Feeling groggy, I pulled on some clothes, put on my polite guest's face, and opened the curtain.

'Good morning,' said the Malindas' daughter. She pointed to a chair, and then withdrew into the back of the house. She returned a few moments later with tea and another plate of salted biscuits. As I drank the tea, washing down the biscuits, Bapak and Ibu Malinda came out to join me.

'We will tell you about Sera,' they said. 'It is important that you know.'

And then, as their daughter refilled my tea glass, they began to list their many miseries. Sera was ridden with violence, they said. The people were not *halus*, not refined. They longed to go back to Yamdena where the people were decent, where they could live in houses with electricity. They had been on Sera for ten years, they said.

'It is a burden,' they said. 'But we do it out of duty.'

I smiled awkwardly. I knew that I too was a burden and a duty.

'You must be careful, *Tuan*,' Bapak Malinda said. 'There are thieves and bad people on the island.'

'Bad people?' I asked.

'On Sera,' he said, 'there are many witches.'

After breakfast, Ibu and Bapak Malinda pointed the way to the house of Matias the sculptor. I walked out into the bright morning and made my way down to the street. I passed the well where the village women were gossiping as they drew water. Children were playing in the dust. Chickens pecked their way to and fro. Dogs were lazing in the shadows of trees – scrawny hunting dogs with mange and protruding ribs, curled up and tired from a night of howling. The women at the well turned and stared. I wished them a good morning. They did not reply.

Matias's house was in the adjacent village, just to the west. Although there were five villages on the northern coast of Sera, the boundaries between them were all but indistinguishable. Together they formed a single stretched-out settlement. As I walked, people came out of their houses to watch me pass.

It took a while asking around before I came to Matias's house. When I arrived, it was obvious I had found the right place. The door, window frames and lintels were carved with crude depictions of suns, angels and crosses. I knocked on the door and looked inside. Matias was sitting in a chair, looking out of the door, and I had the sense that he was waiting for me, that he had been warned of my arrival.

'Come in,' he smiled. 'Sit down.'

'Are you Matias?'

He inclined his head in assent.

I stepped into the dark and he offered a hand. We shook hands, and he introduced himself, pronouncing each syllable of his name: *Ma – ti – as*. There was an empty seat by his side, with a low table between us. He indicated I should sit down. It was all curiously formal. The room was gloomy and the air musty. Little light filtered through the windows.

'I'm pleased to meet you, Matias,' I said. 'Suster Astrid in Saumlaki told me about you.'

He nodded and smiled. 'Ah, yes,' he said. 'Suster Astrid.' He seemed pleased at the mention of her name.

Matias's face was striking. He had a broad, flat nose, and his eyes contained a spark of sharp intelligence as he peered through the thick black rims of his spectacles. His mouth was wide and there was an erratic covering of grey stubble on his cheeks and his chin. As we exchanged pleasantries, he produced a small pair of homemade metal pincers from his pocket. With a theatrical flourish he began to tug at the clumps of stubble, wincing as the hairs came free.

'Shaving,' he explained with a smile. 'This is the best method.'

'You don't have a razor?'

'Why should I need a razor when I have these?' He waved the pincers. 'I made them myself. They are better than any razor.' He paused for a few moments, the pincers aloft. 'I see you know Indonesian. That is good.'

'I am still learning,' I said.

'You know enough,' he said, shifting in his seat. 'We will not have problems.'

There was something awkward about the way he sat, as if he was ill at ease. His bare toes drew patterns in the dust of the floor. Matias's wife came out from the back of the house and put a glass of tea in front of me. The glass was too hot to pick up; it burned my fingertips when I touched it. I left it to cool.

Now that my eyes had adjusted to the light, I could see that in the far corner was a small shrine. On the shrine was an image of the Virgin and Child carved from stone, the forms simple and bold, the features lightly incised.

Matias saw me looking at it. 'That is one of mine,' he said.

'You are Catholic?'

'Yes. I made the sculpture to be bought by the Catholic church, but they said they didn't want it, so now it sits in my house. Go and get it down. Bring it over here.'

I did as he asked, putting the sculpture on the table. Flakes of paint still adhered to the stone.

'Was it once painted?' I asked.

'It was. The church wanted it painted, but when they decided not to buy it, I removed the paint. I prefer it as it is. It is better, don't you think?'

I agreed that it was better. As the tea cooled and as we talked, the room started to fill with onlookers. I told Matias that I was in Sera as a part of a project from the University of Pattimura, and that I had the backing of the Indonesian Institute of Sciences. It seemed important to set out my credentials. He looked unimpressed. I told him I would be in Tanimbar for several months, trying to find out about sculptors who worked in wood and stone.

Matias looked puzzled. 'It is strange that you have come all this way to speak to me about my sculpture,' he said. 'Have they heard of me in England?'

'In England,' I said, 'there are some people who say that the sculptors in Tanimbar are very great, but they do not know the names of any sculptors. I have come to find out more, so I can go home and tell people about your work.' When I said this, I realised it sounded hollow. It was not exactly insincere, but it was dishonest in a way I could not quite put my finger on.

Matias nodded. 'You have come from a university?'

'Yes.'

'And you will go home and write a book?'

'I hope so,' I said. 'One day, yes.'

'Ah,' Matias said. He tugged another clump of hair from his face. 'So you come here for science, for knowledge?'

'Yes.'

'That is good. Science and knowledge are good. But tell me something: when you write your book, will you make any money?'

I felt uneasy. 'A little, perhaps,' I said.

'You will make more than I will,' he said.

I paused. 'Yes,' I said quietly, because he was right. 'But not much.'

He raised his eyebrows. 'You say not much, but I find this strange. I am here in my home in Sera, and I see you, an Englishman, sitting here also, and I think: he can afford to come here. That must cost money. He is sitting in my house in Sera, but I am not sitting in his house in England. This means that he must have more money than I do.'

'Yes,' I said again. *This is not going well*, I thought.

'And I say to myself,' Matias continued, 'if *I* wanted to go to England, could I afford to do that?'

A crowd of onlookers was starting to gather in Matias's house. They seemed fascinated by the Socratic turn the conversation was taking:

'*And would you not say...?*'

'*I would, Socrates.*'

'*Then is it not so that...?*'

'*It is indeed, Socrates.*'

Like one of those unfortunate dupes in Plato's dialogues, I was being led by the nose, an ox ushered to the place of slaughter. Matias's tone was friendly, not particularly hostile, but it was determined.

I took another sip of tea. 'No,' I said quietly. 'I think it would be difficult for you to go to England.'

'Ah,' Matias said with a smile. 'So you can come and go, whilst I must just sit here in my chair.'

Then somebody in the crowd made a joke, a joke that I didn't catch, and everybody laughed. The laughter helped dissipate the growing air of awkwardness. Matias smiled.

'Anyway,' he said, 'you like my sculpture?'

'Yes,' I agreed. 'Very much.'

He nodded. 'I am the greatest sculptor in Tanimbar,' he said. 'Other people may make sculptures, but they do not know history. Only I know history.' He would not be the last person in Tanimbar to tell me this.

'How long have you been working?' I asked him. 'Who was your teacher?'

'Teacher?' Matias looked surprised. 'I had no teacher. That is what makes me greater than the other sculptors you will meet in Tanimbar. Everything you see is my own creation. It comes from my own mind.' Matias tapped the side of his head. Then he put his hand on the Virgin and Child. 'You have seen this sculpture,' he said, 'and it is a demonstration of my art. But I make other sculptures as well, traditional sculptures. I will not show you these yet. I am afraid that these other people will see them.' He pointed to the others in the room and the people crowding around the windows and the door. 'We have lots of time to talk about sculpture, so do not worry. I will tell you lots of things that you can write in your book. But you must be patient.'

Matias looked over at me and smiled. I was beginning to relax again.

'So what was it that made you start sculpting?' I asked.

Matias put the pincers down, then looked at me steadily. 'I sculpt,' he said, 'because I cannot walk.'

It was then I realised the reason for Matias's uncomfortable posture. His legs were twisted where they joined his body. When I looked a little more closely – although not too closely, as it seemed impolite – I saw they were stunted and withered. *I must just sit here in my chair*, I thought.

'What happened?' I asked him.

So Matias told me.

In 1965, just before he was thirty years old, Matias was shinning up a coconut palm. There was a sudden gust of breeze, or a missed footing. He was found in agony at the foot of the tree. He was lucky to still be alive. His family put him on the next boat to Saumlaki. By the time he arrived in the regional capital, it was clear he would never walk again. The Catholic church offered funds to send him to hospital in Ambon.

Matias's trip to Ambon was the only time he had flown, but he was in such pain that he did not have the chance to appreciate the experience. In Ambon, he was collected from the airport by relatives and solicitous members of the church, and he was taken to hospital. They operated on him almost immediately. They did not amputate his legs, but they could do nothing to save the use of them. There was a suggestion that Matias could be sent on to Jakarta, but the risks were too great. This was 1965. Central Indonesia was spiralling into bloodshed and chaos in a series of brutal anti-Communist purges. Even had the political situation been not quite so appalling, it was not clear that the money could have been found. The hospital in Ambon made him as comfortable as they could. When he had recovered sufficiently, they sent him back to Sera, paralysed from the waist down.

Back home, Matias had a wife and child to support. He was no longer able to work on the plantation, to hunt or to fish. They survived on donations and handouts until 1970. These must have been black years for Matias, but eventually he found another livelihood. A lay-worker from the Catholic church by the name of Herman de Vries visited Sera and suggested he start making sculptures to be sold in Ambon. I was to hear more about de Vries in the coming months. He was a shadowy and ambiguous figure – but for Matias, at least, this was a lifeline. This trade in sculpture secured him a scant living. Not only did he sculpt, he also took up goldsmithing. He claimed he had worked out the process of smelting gold himself, and he had never learned anything from anybody.

'Other sculptors,' he said, 'merely copy. But everything I do – my techniques and my ideas – all of these things come from my own mind.'

Matias continued to sculpt until his daughter was old enough to work and provide for him. By the time I met him, he was more or less in retirement. Most of his days were spent drinking palm-wine and playing cards for money, as he smoked clove cigarettes and plucked clumps of beard from his face. He was a skilled – although perhaps not wholly irreproachable – card player. And whilst Matias himself seemed happy to break the tedium of his daily routine to spend time talking with me, over the days that followed, I had the sense that some of his fellow gamblers resented how my presence temporarily put an end to their card games.

Matias's wife appeared around lunchtime with a small plate of food. We continued to talk as we ate. Matias was by turns maudlin, bombastic, good humoured and incisive. It took concentration to follow the conversation, but I realised sometime in the middle of the afternoon that I was enjoying myself. We were developing a rapport. Things were starting to go well after all.

As the sky outside the house darkened, however, Matias seemed to tire.

'That is enough for today. Come back tomorrow,' he said. 'We can talk some more then.' Then he leaned over and with a degree of theatricality pulled out a bag from under the table. The bag clattered as he placed it on the table between us. 'Tomorrow, maybe, I will show you my traditional sculptures,' he said. He paused. 'Or perhaps I will decide not to show you,' he said.

'I'd like to see them,' I said.

'Maybe. But I'm afraid.'

'Afraid? Why?'

'These sculptures come from my own imagination, my own mind. They are *my* sculptures.' He patted the bag.

'Yes, I know.'

'I'm afraid that you will steal them.'

The accusation was unexpected. I felt a surge of affronted indignation. 'No,' I said. 'Of course I am not here to steal.'

Matias held up his hand. He spoke softly. 'I do not think that you have come to steal with the hands,' he said. 'I am afraid that you have come to steal with the eyes.'

Matias's gaze was steady. I looked away guiltily.

Curi mata: stealing with the eyes. The accusation was inescapable. What else did Westerners do, the whole world over, if not this? They roved here and there, taking other people's lives and homes as things to be photographed, consumed, ferried back home. Wasn't anthropology itself no more than a vast enterprise of stealing with the eyes? Wasn't the entire world, under the guise of knowledge and science, a cabinet of curiosity for the West?

I wanted to speak up in my defence. I wanted to say I was here for knowledge, and knowledge was for everyone. I wanted to protest that this was humankind's shared heritage. I wanted to reassure Matias of my good intentions. But I knew this was sophistry. Knowledge was unevenly distributed across the world. Anything that I ended up writing would be of scant use to Matias back there in Sera. I would come and go – stealing with my eyes and ears – as many others had come and gone. And he would still be stuck there in Tanimbar. *What the fuck am I doing?* I thought, not for the first or the last time.

'I'm sorry,' I said to Matias. 'If you do not want to show me...'

'I am not saying I will not show you,' he said. 'But you need to know how things are. Come back tomorrow. We can talk some more.'

'Thank you,' I said.

I stood and shook Matias's hand. He looked amused as I said goodbye. I nodded to the men who were clustered around the door, and stepped out into the cool evening air.

6

THREE TIMES

The following morning, feeling like I could do with some time by myself, I headed down to the beach to sketch the boats awaiting high tide. A cluster of kids gathered behind me, laughing and joking. A couple of fishermen were getting ready to put out to sea. On the horizon to the north, I could see Selu, the isle of the dead. I was uneasy about returning to Matias's house, uncomfortable with his accusations of the previous afternoon. My reluctance was compounded by the fact that Ibu and Bapak Malinda had discussed the matter of my visiting Matias, and had told me the night before that they did not think I should spend any more time with the sculptor.

'He is a bad man,' Ibu Malinda said. 'He is a gambler, and he drinks too much.'

Perhaps they were trying to get rid of me, to send me back to Saumlaki early. But I didn't take the hint. I said I had work to do, and Matias was expecting me. They shrugged in resignation.

'Well,' they said, 'it is important that you know these things.'

That morning, I decided to leave my camera at home. It was intrusive to turn up with a camera. I wanted to reassure Matias of my good intentions. And – what was perhaps harder – I wanted to reassure *myself* of my good intentions. This was, in large part, where the problem lay. After my Socratic conversation of the day before, I was filled with doubts and uncertainties. Good or bad, I was not at all sure what my intentions were.

I finished sketching, and put away my sketchbook and pencils. Then I stood up, shooed away the kids and headed up the street to see the sculptor. When I arrived at his house, Matias did not seem to be expecting me. Although it was still early, there was a small knot of men in the front room, playing cards and drinking. It was never too early to start drinking palm-wine in Tanimbar. But even if my arrival was unexpected, it did not seem to be unwelcome. Matias beamed and waved me into the house. His companions grumbled as they cleared away the cards and sloped out into the street.

'So,' said Matias, 'you have come back.'

'I have come back.'

'I am pleased. I did not know if you would return. Would you like tea?'

'Yes, thanks.'

Matias was polite, almost conciliatory, after the previous day's criticism. It struck me then that his life must have been almost unbearably monotonous, that however unsettling my intrusion, however great his mistrust, I was at least a novelty, and the fact that I was coming to see *him*, of all the people on Sera, conferred upon him a certain status.

The last of his companions disappeared off into the sunlight, and we sat either side of the small table. From underneath, Matias pulled out the mysterious cloth bag he had shown me the previous day and placed it on the tabletop. His wife brought tea. Matias and I made small talk. Was I enjoying my time in Sera? How long would I be staying? Was it better than Saumlaki, or worse? Perhaps it was because today he did not have an audience, but Matias was much less bombastic. He seemed determined to play the part of the perfect host.

When we had finished our tea, Matias asked me if I had brought my camera. I said no. I had come only to talk. I told him I had a sketchbook, and showed him my picture of the beach. He looked unimpressed. Then he put his hand into the cloth bag and pulled out a small white object, placing it on the table between us. It was a tiny sculpture, carved from a tooth. He said it was the tooth of a dugong. The figure could not have been more than ten centimetres in height. It sat erect, knees drawn up, its buttocks resting on its heels. It held a bowl in its tiny hands. A small tail curved up the creature's back. But it was the little beast's face that was most striking. Above the two rows of lightly incised teeth, bared in a skull-like grin, was a snub nose, and on either side of the nose stared two hypnotic saucer eyes. From the creature's head protruded a pair of small horns.

Matias was looking very pleased with himself.

'Can I have a closer look?' I asked him. The lingering mistrust of the day before made me careful, respectful. The sculptor wordlessly picked up the figure and put it into my hand. It was smooth and cool.

'One of yours?' I asked.

Matias nodded.

'Is it a devil?' I asked, putting the sculpture gently back down on the table.

'No,' he said, 'it is not a devil.' He put out his hand for the sculpture. I handed it back to him, and he let it rest in his broad palm, feeling its weight. *'It is a human being not yet perfected,'* he said.

☓

Over the next couple of days, I saw more of Matias's sculptures. He would pull them one by one from his bag to show me. The workmanship of many of these sculptures was crude, but there was something compelling about them. In their sheer variety, they seemed the product of a wild, perhaps desperate, imagination. One large wooden sculpture had devils' horns and huge, erect genitals, its lips pulled back in a lecherous sneer. Another smaller piece, carved out of soft stone, looked like a frightened monkey, curled in on itself in terror with hunched shoulders and bulging eyes, the head jutting out watchfully. Still others had tails, or several heads. Perhaps the most fantastic of all was a carved pillar around which clustered nine heads, the largest of which wore a brutal, leering smile. Where the largest head should have had ears, there sprouted instead a pair of wings. Matias showed me each one for a few minutes, then he hid the sculptures away again in his cloth bag, or under the ikat cloths stowed beneath the table, as if these poor creatures vampirically could not bear to be exposed to too much daylight. Each time I asked what the sculptures depicted, Matias gave the same answer: they were *manusia belum sempurna*, human beings not yet perfected.

'Why do you sculpt these things?' I asked him one day, thinking about his own broken body, his disfigurement, the frustration of being pinned to his chair there in Sera.

'In the old days,' he said, 'that is how things were in Tanimbar. Human beings were not yet perfected. Who knows why, but this is how things were.'

A few onlookers had gathered again, and were listening in on our conversation. They murmured in agreement as if to say *yes, yes, this was indeed how things were.*

'People in Tanimbar used to have horns?'

Matias looked at me without smiling. 'There were some with horns,' he said. 'Some had many heads, or no heads. Some had eyes in their chests or wings or tails. But now, you see, things are different.' He pointed to the others in the room. 'Now we people in Tanimbar are fully human.' A couple of the onlookers grinned.

Another man joined in the discussion, a well-dressed young man sitting by the door, perhaps a university student back from Ambon to see his family. 'Back then,' he said, giving the conversation a Darwinian twist, 'human beings were still monkeys. But now we are fully human. Now we are Christian. Now we wear trousers.'

Matias broke in again. 'Get out your book and write this down,' he said. 'I will tell you how it was. First there was the *jaman purba*, the ancient age when people were unperfected. This is what life was like then, everything mixed up, humans and animals and monkeys.' He gestured towards the bag of sculptures. 'These are the things I make, to show people how things were. The people's bodies were imperfect and jumbled. Everything was unclear.'

As I scribbled notes, I thought of the world before Atuf, the time when land and sea, male and female, earth and sky, sun and moon were not yet split apart, a time of chaos, when those things that should be unmixed were mixed.

'And then?' I asked.

'After that was the *jaman pertengahan,* the middle ages. In this time, people were perfect in their bodies, but they did not know religion. This was the time of our Tanimbarese tradition, the time of *adat.*'

The man who had talked about monkeys and trousers spoke up again. 'After that,' he said, 'religion came to Tanimbar, and now we are Christian.'

Matias nodded. 'Yes, this is the *jaman moderen*, this is the modern age. Now we are Christian.'

The other man elaborated. 'It was like this. In ancient times, people went about naked. In traditional times they wore loincloths and bird-of-paradise feathers in their hair. But now we here in Tanimbar are modern, we wear trousers and we worship God.'

It was a neat genealogy. First unredeemed bodies and minds, then bodies redeemed and minds unredeemed, then both bodies and minds redeemed. Nakedness, then loincloths, then trousers.

I indicated the bag of sculptures. 'What happened to end the ancient age?' I asked. 'What happened to these human beings not yet perfected?'

Matias shrugged. 'Who knows?' he said. 'Perhaps they married people who were already perfected, or perhaps they just died out, deep in the forests.'

'Or perhaps there are still some left?' I asked.

Matias frowned. 'No,' he said, 'I think that there are no more of them.'

The other man spoke again. 'The last one died in 1910,' he said.

The date seemed significant: the year the Christian missions arrived in Tanimbar. I wondered if this was coincidental. 'Why did they die out?' I asked.

Matias shook his head. 'I don't know,' he said. 'This is just what happened, I do not know how. But sometimes even now children are born who are strange. And when this happens, this reminds us how things were in the *jaman purba*.'

'Like a mother giving birth to an octopus?' I asked.

'Yes,' Matias said. 'These *barang aneh* come from the *jaman purba*.'

For Tanimbar was still a place where buffalo gave birth to monstrous calves and women to inhuman children, where God and the ancestors struggled to make their voices heard. *Jaman purba, jaman pertengahan* and *jaman moderen* – it was not so much that these were successive ages of history. It was more that they were different *possibilities of being* that overlapped, swirled together, collided with each other. Out of the maelstrom of these different times and possibilities, the present was born and reborn.

$$\text{\Lightning}$$

That evening, after concluding the business of the day with Matias, I was sitting outside with a couple of old men from the village. Hanging over Sera was a fat quarter moon, lying rolled onto its back in the deepening blue of the sky. The night air was scented with the fragrance of the clove cigarettes that both of my companions were smoking. As we sat talking, one of the men pointed to the moon.

'They say that people from the West have been to the moon,' he said. 'Is it true?'

'Yes,' I said.

'What did they find there?'

'Oh, nothing much. Only rock.'

He laughed. 'Only rock? They went all the way to the moon and only found rock?'

'Yes,' I agreed.

'All that way?'

'All that way,' I said.

The old man tutted. 'They could have come to Tanimbar,' he said, kicking a stone. 'If they wanted rock they could have come to Tanimbar.'

'Well,' I said, 'they used to think the moon was made of cheese, so they went to check. But when they got there they saw it was only rock.'

He gave a half smile, as if he did not quite disbelieve me, but was certainly not prepared to believe me either.

'That,' I explained, 'is what they say in England, that the moon is made of cheese. But now they know it is only rock.'

'It must be expensive to go to the moon,' the old man said, ignoring my reference to cheese as the distraction it was.

'It's expensive enough coming to Tanimbar, let alone the moon,' I replied.

He laughed. Then the other man leaned over and offered me a cigarette. When I refused, he looked reproachful. 'You cannot become Tanimbarese unless you smoke,' he said. He turned to his friend. 'You know,' he said, 'it was the Americans. It was the Americans who went to the moon. They went in Apollo 11. Do you know what Apollo means?'

We both shook our heads.

'*A*-merika *POL*-itik,' he said. He paused for effect. '*A*-merika *POL*-itik number eleven. That is why they went to the moon. Not for rock, but for politics.'

'Whether they go for rock or whether they go for politics,' his friend said, pulling on a cigarette, 'it is a bad thing to go to the moon. People should not do these things.'

Then he sighed, and the conversation took a strange turn.

'What do you think will happen?' he asked me, pulling on his cigarette.

'To what?' I asked.

'To this world.'

I shrugged. I was not sure I understood what he meant.

'In the year 2000?' he said. 'What will happen to this world in the year 2000?'

'Maybe it will not be much different from now,' I said.

He shook his head gravely. 'No, it will be different. Everything will be different. In the year 2000, everything will be finished. This world will be no more.' He was staring up at the moon, sucking on the remnant of his cigarette. Then he dropped it to the ground and stubbed it out with his heel. 'It will be the end of suffering and sin. It is written in the Bible.'

His friend turned to me. 'You do not believe this?' he asked.

'No,' I said. 'I do not believe it.'

The two men laughed. 'You people from the West may have been to the moon, but you don't believe anything any more. Anyway, you will soon find out. There is not long to wait.'

A couple of days later, things between Matias and myself became more complicated. One afternoon, just as I was leaving, he made me an offer. He would let me see his sculptures, he said – he would let me photograph them, would let me see how he made them, would even teach me his craft – but I would have to pay. Matias told me he had asked around the village to discover the going rate for a term's study at the University of Pattimura in Ambon, and he had a proposal to put to me: if I would pay him the equivalent cost of a term's study, I could stay in Sera and become his disciple. In return, he would teach me everything he knew. Then I could go back and tell the world about it. And, on top of that, I could photograph anything that I liked.

'You will learn things that you cannot learn in any university,' he said. 'You will learn how to carve bone and tooth and stone and wood, and you will learn how to smelt gold.'

I hesitated. Then I told him I did not want to learn to make sculptures myself. Instead, I was interested in the sculptures that *he* made. Besides, I said, I did not have the kind of money he was asking for. This was true: I was on a tight budget. But Matias refused to believe me. Not unreasonably, he surmised that if I had the money to come to Tanimbar at all, my supplies of money must be almost infinite.

'Do not make a decision now,' he said. 'Come back tomorrow and we can talk then.'

The next day, when I returned to Matias's house, he was waiting for me, the bag of sculptures on the table. I sat down, his wife brought us tea, and I told him that I was sorry, but I did not wish to be his disciple. I could not afford the time or the money, I said.

Matias sighed, but he did not look surprised. Then he took the bag and put it under the table. 'In that case,' he said, 'let us talk about other matters.'

We drank tea and we talked about other things. And then I asked Matias a question I now regret. I told him how, a few nights before, I had fallen into conversation with two men, and we had talked about the moon mission, and the Americans, and the future, and the year 2000.

'Matias,' I asked him, 'what do you think will happen in the year 2000?'

Matias smiled, looking a little sad, and he said, 'It is there in the Bible. It is not a matter of what I think. In the year 2000, the sick will be made to walk and the poor will be made rich. I will walk around the village again; my legs will be healed.' He pointed down at his shattered legs, hope in his eyes, and I knew then that the story he had told me of *jaman purba* and *jaman pertengahan* and *jaman moderen* was still incomplete. Sometime soon, this struggle in Tanimbar – between the new gods of church and state, the old ancestors and the ancient forces of chaos – would be over. Bodies and souls would be perfected and there would be trousers for everyone. It would be the inauguration of a new Heaven and a new Earth. The Holy City, the New Jerusalem, would appear, decked out like a bride coming to meet her bridegroom.

'You will walk again?' I asked.

'Yes,' Matias said. 'That is what I believe.'

ϗ

I spent another few days in Sera, but Matias was running out of patience with me. Our conversations were beginning to turn in on themselves, moving in a circular fashion without going anywhere new. Matias was becoming bored, and yet he continued to talk, because talking was at least better than the tedium of a life pinned to his chair – and besides, whilst I was still there he could perhaps tell himself there was hope I might be able to offer him something more concrete to ease the passage of those long six years until the coming of the New Jerusalem. But in the end, when I said I was leaving, he looked relieved.

'You must take a photograph of me,' he said. 'You do not have a photograph of the sculptures, but I do not want you to leave Sera empty handed. Take a photograph, and go back and tell people that Matias is a great sculptor. Then perhaps others will come.'

I photographed him in his chair, staring straight at the camera. Then I wished him well, and I left his house for the final time.

As for Bapak and Ibu Malinda, I had thought they would be glad to see the back of me, but I misjudged them. When I told them I was leaving, they told me how much they had enjoyed having my company; then they put on a fine feast for my final evening. We sat talking until late, and they gave me messages to relay back to friends and family in Saumlaki.

The following morning, they gave me a farewell breakfast and wished me well. Bapak Malinda took me down to the shore. The beach was crowded. The men of the village were preparing for an expedition in search of sea cucumber, which they were going to sell to raise money for the building of a new Protestant church. They would be away for several days. As a Catholic, Bapak Malinda had no obligations to join their number. He more or less ignored them as he waded out to where his dugout was moored. I followed with my bag on my back and got on board. Bapak Malinda rowed me towards a boat that was waiting a little way out to sea. The boat's owners, Makassarese traders, had agreed to take me back to Saumlaki. Bapak Malinda clasped my hand as he said goodbye, with a genuine warmth I had not seen in him before. I thanked him again and scrambled aboard. The boat was a far sleeker vessel than the one by means of which I had arrived, with smooth lines and reassuring air of seaworthiness. The traders had little interest in me. They left me to my own devices. I sat up in the bows of the boat and watched Bapak Malinda paddle back to shore. The first of the assembled boats was putting out to sea in search of the sea cucumber that would pass through many hands before, perhaps, landing on the tables of gourmets in Shanghai or Beijing. The engine started and we headed east, following the line of the northern coast of Sera.

It was a beautiful, clear day. The water was a deep blue, shot through with the gold of the sun. There was not even a trace of cloud in the sky, and the stiff breeze prevented the morning becoming too hot. Down in the water, shoals of pulsating jellyfish hung motionless, like the ghosts of fish. After I had spent a couple of hours lounging in the bows, the traders hailed me for lunch, which they cooked on deck on a small Primus stove: fish, rice and noodles. We ate in silence. Having eaten, I headed back up to the front of the boat, relishing the solitude after days of constant company.

Back in Saumlaki, we put into dock at the end of the jetty. I thanked the traders. They refused to let me pay for the lift. And then I walked back through the plaza to the Lovely Hope hotel.

7

ANCHORAGES

The Harapan Indah was almost deserted. The other guests had left, the construction crew headed north to work on the road that wound up the east coast of Yamdena and the Sumbawanese newlywed gone who-knows-where. I unpacked my bags, had a shower, then ordered a beer. I sat alone at the back of the hotel looking out to sea. I watched the lights of the fishing boats glinting in the growing dark, the columns of smoke rising from the forests almost vertically up to the sky, and wondered about the long obsession that had led me to the Tanimbar Islands, the strange mania that had driven me halfway around the world so that I could steal with the eyes.

Over a month had passed since I had left home, and since my departure – this was in the days before electronic communications pervaded everywhere like an invisible, suffocating gas – I had not had any contact with anybody. I felt lonely, but also relished my loneliness. There was a strange pleasure in this knowledge that I was cut off and adrift, because as I settled into my isolation I realised that there was nothing of urgency to be done, there were no demands upon me: I was simply there, looking at the evening sky, feeling the realities upon which I once relied drift and scatter, as fragile and insubstantial as the columns of smoke rising from the trees across the bay.

But then, when I looked up, I saw something that made me shudder with unease. A light appeared from over the forests near the village of Olilit Baru. It moved steadily southwards, heading into the face of the wind, arcing over my head in the direction of the island of Selaru. It moved steadily until it was lost over the trees.

A satellite, of course. What else could it be? But when, a couple of days later, I told a Tanimbarese friend about the strange light, he looked at me without saying anything for a few moments. Then he said, '*Tuan*, let me tell you: what you saw was a witch.'

People in Saumlaki frequently referred to the village of Olilit Baru, from where the light had seemed to emerge, as *neraka*, or hell. It was a pleasant, friendly village; later it became my home. But it had a poor reputation. It was named after hell because it was said to be hot with the dangerous power of witchcraft. Often, my Tanimbarese friend said, you could see witches flying back and forth from Olilit Baru, riding high in the sky with paraffin lamps in their hands. They went north to Ambon to buy cheap beer, and south to Selaru where they gathered in large numbers for nefarious purposes. The soul of a Tanimbarese witch is an insubstantial thing, entirely without anchor. This is why witches can fly, and why they can enter the bodies of their enemies, where they cause sickness or even death.

But it is a terrible thing to be a witch, to be without any anchorage. For a soul without ballast, the world is terrifying. Cut adrift, witches crave trinkets and shiny things. They are driven, like compulsive shoppers, to accumulate anything that might lend them weight and grant them refuge in the turbulent seas of existence. This acquisitiveness makes them dangerous. Whatever you have – your gold earrings, your tape recorder, your camera – they want. If they see you own something desirable, they will attempt to take it from you, through flattery or deceit. And if you do not co-operate, they will slip into your body when you are inattentive and gnaw at your entrails until you relinquish whatever it is they long for. But the tragedy of the witch is this: the objects they desire are no more capable of anchoring their insubstantial souls than can a boat be made fast with an anchor made of balsa wood.

During the nights that followed, I kept watch on the skies for further lights flying from Olilit Baru to Selaru – but I didn't see any. Nevertheless, sometimes, in those early days in Tanimbar, as I was buffeted here and there across the islands, lonely and unanchored, in search of significance and weight, I wondered if I myself were part witch.

I spent the following days in Saumlaki making connections, planning where to head next, trying to accumulate weight. I felt bruised from my encounter with Matias, unable to answer his accusation that I was stealing with the eyes. I had become suspicious of my own motives, uneasy with what I was doing in Tanimbar. I was not sure whether this poking around in other people's lives did anything other than increase their stores of dissatisfaction and unhappiness.

But then Benny Fenyapwain called by on his motorbike, full of enthusiasm and good cheer, and I felt better about things. He wanted to know about Sera, and about my encounter with Matias.

He shrugged when I talked about Matias's accusation against me. 'He doesn't understand,' Benny said quietly.

I hoped that he was right, even if I could not put my discomfort to one side so easily. Then Benny suggested that we head up the coast for a short trip to the village of Sangliat Dol, where he had relatives. Sangliat Dol was perhaps the most famous of all Tanimbarese villages. Then, as now, tourism in Tanimbar was a pretty scratchy affair, and the islands attracted no more than a handful of visitors each month. But to the extent that there was a tourist industry in Tanimbar at all, Sangliat Dol was one of the major tourist sites, famous for the crumbling monument at the heart of the village: a stone boat, or *natar* in the Yamdenan language.

The *natar* in Sangliat Dol reflected the deep past of Tanimbar's history, the point at which the *jaman purba* gave way to the *jaman pertengahan*. In the period after Atuf speared the sun, the Tanimbar Islands were plunged into chaos and upheaval. With the sun careering across the sky, and time now set in motion, populations were set adrift, whole villages tossed to and fro like boats in a storm. It was a time of plagues, floods and epidemics. Witches, feeding off the chaos, flourished. It took great heroes to re-anchor the world by travelling to other realms to bring back gold, because only gold is heavy enough to act as ballast in the seas of disorder. Amongst the heroes whose names are still known is So'u Melatunan, who negotiated a passage on the sailing ships of the colonists, and who tricked the foreigners out of their gold. There is also Itran Rumaenga, who plunged into the underworld and stole gold earrings from a group of children. He had the foresight to swallow the purloined jewellery. When the outraged children apprehended him and subjected him to a strip-search, they found nothing. The hero made his escape and, the following day, he excreted the gold.

Amidst the surging seas of chaos, anchored by the weight of gold, villagers started to gather and settle. In some places, they built stone boats as powerful symbols of how they could ride out the waves and tides of uncertainty and change. Buried beneath the boats were clutches of the gold that had been wrested from other worlds.

Firmly rooted, solid and heavy, the *natar* is the antithesis of rootlessness and flux. It is the exact opposite of the flightiness of witches. It is here that the village gathers, to dance as Atuf and Inkelu once danced, to discuss important business, to negotiate exchanges, to perform rituals and ceremonies, to cut new passages through the waters of time and history. Village halls and meeting places in Tanimbar continue to be called *natar*, because they too are stone boats, places where the village can gather and set a course to the future, whilst remaining anchored in the past. The monument in Sangliat Dol was one of the last remaining of its kind. I was keen to see it.

✕

Benny suggested we take the bus, so one weekend morning we met at the hotel, walked down to Yamdena Plaza, bought some fried peanuts and fruit for the journey and then squeezed on board the bus. A sign on the side of the vehicle read 'Duty is Happiness'. This struck me as not invariably true. We munched on peanuts as the bus filled with passengers. When it was almost impossibly full, the bus crawled out of the plaza and turned into the road.

Our progress northwards was accompanied by the relentless sentimentalism of Ambonese pop music, played at distorting volume on the bus stereo. I had seen the videos on TV in Ambon: music sung by damp-eyed and earnest young men, dressed in Hawaiian shirts, swaying and clicking their fingers on the beach against a backdrop of dugout canoes and palm trees, singing in close harmony '*Satu tetes air susu, mama...*' ('One drop of your milk, mother...') – a ballad about longing for home, in a place almost entirely innocent of Freud and his Oedipal suspicions.

We took the bus as far as the village of Amdasa. 'We'll get out here,' Benny said. 'We can head down to the beach and walk around the coast to Sangliat Dol. Then we can arrive in the village by the steps. It is much more impressive.'

We got out of the bus. A crowd of kids clustered around us. Seeing my white face, they called out, 'Hello, Pastor! Hello, Pastor!' I waved at them in friendly, but noncommittal, benediction.

Benny grinned. 'These kids think that all foreigners are priests,' he said. He shooed them away.

Ϫ

We walked along the beach, following the coast towards Sangliat Dol. The breezes coming off the sea cooled the air, and the sand was a beautiful, pure white. We picked our way through a thicket of mangroves, and Benny warned me to watch out for snakes. As we walked, we discussed philosophy and religion and all the things that Benny was interested in talking about. It was a relief to have an ally in Tanimbar, somebody who shared my enthusiasms. My anxiety started to ebb away. Perhaps, I thought, my presence there could be justified after all.

Eventually we came to the steps that led up to the clifftop village, where there was a carnival atmosphere: the village women, along with a ragtag gaggle of kids, were out with their machetes weeding the steep stone staircase. They called out in greeting and asked if I had a camera. I said that I had.

'Well, you must take a photograph of us,' they said.

I pulled my camera out of my bag and took a picture.

Putting the camera away, I asked the village women what they were up to.

'Sangliat Dol is a tourist village,' they said. 'We are making it look good for the tourists.'

'Do you get many tourists?' I asked.

'Yes,' they said. 'Every week now we have five or six. But when the village is improved, we will have more. This is progress.'

After my return from Tanimbar, that photo lay forgotten for more than a decade and a half. But then, one day, I came across a website belonging to a cruise company. This company, based in Australia, was advertising an expensive cruise, the highlight of which would be a visit to the 'untouched' village of Sangliat Dol. The somewhat breathless prose on the website assured travellers that that people in Sangliat Dol had never even met any Westerners before. Thinking that the owners of the cruise line might appreciate it, I sent them a copy of the photograph, accompanied by a note explaining that, over fifteen years before, I had come across this cheerful scene of local village women sprucing up their village for Western tourists.

The cruise company did not reply, but neither did they update their website.

We climbed the steps up to the village. As we emerged at the top, we could see Sangliat Dol's famous stone boat bearing towards us. It was an impressive sight: a great stone platform twenty yards long, with a carved prow board lashed to the front with rope and twine, like a stone version of the *kora ulu*, or wooden prow boards, that were once attached to the front of Tanimbarese war canoes. The boat was cross-hatched with graffiti. I took out my camera.

'You can take photographs later,' said Benny. 'But if you want to take a photograph, you'll have to pay.'

'Who do I pay?'

'The village authorities,' he said. 'If you are Tanimbarese, or even just Indonesian you can give a bottle of palm-wine for the ancestors, and then take a photograph. But these days they ask foreigners to pay in rupiah.'

I put my camera back in my bag, intending to sort out payment later.

'This place is very hot,' Benny said. 'It is hot with *adat* heat. That is why you have to pay. If we take photographs and do not make offerings to the ancestors, we will be in trouble. It is said that there is gold buried underneath the prow of the boat. The gold makes the boat hot. So we must be careful.'

I was going to ask him more, but then we were spotted by a group of kids who ran over and clustered around, shouting, 'Hello, Pastor! Hello, Pastor!'

'Come on,' said Benny, 'let's go and have some tea.' He led me to his relatives' house and they invited me in for tea. Outside the kids clustered around the windows, peering inside and giggling.

I have always loved the paradox of the stone boat. It is a symbol that stands at the meeting place of land and sea, one that encompasses both fixity and movement. After he was executed, it is said that Saint James travelled to Spain in a miraculous stone boat with the help of neither sails nor oars. In the Celtic world, there are myths of giants and saints putting to sea in vessels made of stone. And there are glimpses of similar tales everywhere from China to Egypt. More recently, the philosopher Gaston Bachelard, lying in his bed in Paris, listened to the traffic noise outside and allowed himself reveries of the sea and of the storm, imagining that his bed was being tossed on the waves. 'I talk to myself to give myself cheer,' he wrote. 'There now, your skiff is holding its own, you are safe in your stone boat'.

Over tea, we talked about sculpture and stone boats. Benny's relatives were cordial and hospitable. When I asked about photographing the boat, they shrugged.

'These days,' they said, 'they ask tourists for too much money. You can take a photograph if you like, but it is better not to.'

I decided to take their advice. So, instead, I asked them if there were any sculptors in Sangliat Dol. They said that they didn't know of any. But there was, they said, a sculptor up the coast, in the village of Alusi Krawain. His name was Abraham Amelwatin. His brother lived in Saumlaki, and worked as a schoolteacher.

'I have seen Abraham's sculptures,' Benny said. 'He is a very great artist. Perhaps you can go and see him some time. I'll introduce you to his brother, Pak Isak. He teaches science in the high school in Saumlaki.'

Towards the middle of the afternoon, it became clear that our hosts had other things to be doing, and so Benny and I decided to head back. We could have caught the bus direct from Sangliat Dol, but Benny said he preferred to walk. So we thanked his relations and walked back down the steps. We headed along the beaches and through the mangroves until we arrived in Amdasa, where a bus was waiting to take us back to Saumlaki.

PART III

JAMAN PERTENGAHAN

THE AGE OF THE ANCESTORS

Abraham Amelwatin, from Alusi Krawain, Yamdena

8

WHISTLIN' PAST THE GRAVEYARD

A few days later, Benny introduced me to Pak Isak Amelwatin, Abraham's brother. He was a slightly corpulent figure with curly black hair, dressed in the drab grey of a government official. I spoke with him at the school, and he invited me to come back to his house on the outskirts of Saumlaki later in the day. He told me that it was easy to find: I only had to walk out of town and stop by the first house on the right with a papaya tree outside the door.

'I have some sculptures made by my brother,' he said. 'They are very fine sculptures, very traditional. I am sure they will interest you.'

I found the house without difficulty. Pak Isak was waiting for me on the balcony, sitting in the shade of the papaya, looking like a man who was enjoying his afternoon off. He rose from his seat, came to shake my hand and invited me in. He made me tea and, once he had done so, he took from his cupboard three sculptures carefully wrapped in ikat cloths. He unwound the cloths one by one, folded them and placed the sculptures on the ground in front of me. Two of the sculptures were warrior figures in headcloths and loincloths. The third figure was both strange and compelling: a female likeness that seemed to owe more than a passing debt to the Buddhist and Hindu sculptures of Java and Bali – she looked to me like a Tanimbarese avatar of the bodhisattva Avalokiteshvara. She had four arms and a headdress, and around her neck there hung a pendant with the form of a buffalo head. Her head was haloed by a striking series of swirling flourishes like rolling waves. I immediately thought of the sculptures of Tanimbar's past, of the *kora ulu* or prow boards and the household altarpieces I had seen in museums in the West.

Pak Isak pointed at the warriors. 'These two,' he said, 'are Tanimbarese warriors. This is what our ancestors were like.'

'And the other?' I asked, pointing at the haloed woman.

'The other,' he said, 'is a witch.'

Given that Pak Isak was a science teacher, I thought I would take the opportunity to ask him about witchcraft. 'She is very beautiful.' I said. 'Can I pick her up?'

He nodded.

I held the witch in my hands. Then I looked at Pak Isak and asked, as lightly as I could, 'Are there still witches in Tanimbar?'

Pak Isak hesitated. He seemed unsure of what to say, as if his scientifically trained mind was wrestling with his Tanimbarese heart. 'No,' he said slowly, although not without an air of uncertainty, 'I don't think so. There were once, in the past. But not any more.'

'They say there are still witches in Olilit Baru,' I said. 'They call it *neraka*, or hell.'

Pak Isak paused. 'I know,' he said. 'But I do not believe it. There are no witches any more.'

'What happened to them?'

Pak Isak shrugged. 'They died out.'

Just like that. They died out. 'Why?' I asked.

He thought for a moment. 'Before we knew religion, there were still witches in Tanimbar. But now that we are Christian, there are no more witches.'

I thought about telling Pak Isak about the light I had seen arcing across the sky from Olilit Baru to Selaru, but I decided against it. Then Pak Isak changed the subject, as if all this talk of witchcraft made him uncomfortable. He took the sculpture of the witch from me.

'These two are noblemen,' he explained, drawing my attention to the warrior figures. 'In the past, we Tanimbarese were strong, handsome people. But now we are short and fat.' He patted his belly and chuckled. It was true that Pak Isak did not much resemble the Tanimbarese warriors described a century before by Henry Ogg Forbes as 'handsome-featured fellows, lithe, tall, erect, and with splendidly formed bodies'. Pak Isak frowned for a moment. Then he said, 'Things have now changed. We are no longer so strong or so handsome. In those days, people ate better food. The air and the sea were clean. Now they are dirty. These days there are too many chemicals.'

We sat in silence for a while. 'What are you going to do with these sculptures?' I asked.

'I have sold them to a man from Ambon. But you should go to see my brother Abraham. He will help you. He will tell you about all these things, about the history of Tanimbar.'

Ϫ

I decided I should go and visit Abraham in Alusi Krawain, and so I started making arrangements for my departure. The day after speaking to Pak Isak, I caught up with Suster Astrid and Ibu Neli in the school offices. When she heard I was heading north again, Suster Astrid offered to write me a letter of recommendation. She knew a couple who lived in Alusi Krawain and said they would be good hosts.

'I have helped them in the past, so they will be certain to help you. You will be comfortable there. They are good people.' Suster Astrid looked around for a piece of paper and a pen, and began to scribble something down for me. She folded the paper neatly so that it formed its own envelope, and wrote an address on the front. 'Ibu Lin and Bapak Rerebain,' it read. 'Alusi Krawain Village, Tanimbar.'

I put the note in my pocket and thanked her.

'Remember,' Suster Astrid advised me, 'when you go to the village, go straight to that address. Do not go anywhere else, because you might get into trouble.'

I bade her goodbye, and she shook my hand warmly.

'Come back and visit us again,' she said. 'I will be expecting you. I will want to hear about your adventures. I think you will like Alusi Krawain. It is a very nice village on the clifftop. Lots of cool breeze.'

She led me to the school gate. As I left, she slapped me gently on the back. 'Make sure you are careful,' she said with a smile. 'We don't want you coming to any harm. What would we tell your family back in England?'

Ϫ

The following day, I caught the bus north again. We crawled along the road out of town, through Sangliat Dol and onwards towards the north. It was slow going. Several hours after our departure we reached the village of Arui Das, some five miles south of Alusi Krawain. At Arui Das, the road was blocked. There was a small gully that carried a stream down to the sea, and the bridge over the gully had collapsed. The bus driver said he could go no further. We all climbed out. The bus hooted its horn, gathering passengers for the journey back to the south.

As I wondered what to do next, a young man holding a knife lurched towards me. He put his arm around my shoulders, and I could smell palm-wine on his breath.

'English?' he asked, his speech slurred.

I said that I was. He lifted his knife. The blade gleamed in the sun. Then he wobbled and said, in a comradely fashion, 'Welcome to Arui Das.'

I heard somebody laugh. I looked round to see a thin, middle-aged man in shorts and dark glasses.

'Don't worry about him,' he said. 'He's just drunk. He's not angry.'

The man with the knife swayed again, and started to protest his sobriety.

The other man ignored him. 'What are you doing in Arui Das?' he asked. 'Are you a tourist?'

'No, I'm heading to Alusi Krawain,' I said. 'I've been given an address by Suster Astrid in Saumlaki.'

At the mention of the nun's name, he became appreciably warmer. 'Suster Astrid – ah, good. If you are going to Alusi Krawain, I should be able to help you. Please, come with me.'

The man with the knife still had his arm around my shoulders. He looked at me blearily and waved the knife in front of my nose.

'Let's go,' I said to him. And so the three of us made our shambling way down the street.

When we arrived at my host's house, he dismissed my knife-wielding companion, who took his arm from my shoulder and shuffled off with a sullen look on his face.

'He's always drunk,' my host said as he poured the tea. 'Who are you going to visit in Alusi Krawain?'

I pulled Suster Astrid's letter from my pocket and passed it to him. He read the address.

'Ibu Lin and Bapak Rerebain? I know them. They are good people. If you want to go north there are two possibilities. Either you can walk, which will take a little while, or I can take you. I have a boat, and we can go up the coast. It will be more convenient, I think.'

'You are not busy?'

He grinned. 'I am not very busy,' he said. 'I have some business in Alusi Krawain myself, so it is no trouble.'

When we had finished tea, we went down to the beach. My host untied an outrigger canoe and pushed it out into the shallows. I rolled up my trousers and followed him, my backpack on my back. I tossed the backpack into the boat and climbed in. Soon we were out in the bay, the sea floor falling rapidly away beneath us, the water sparkling and clear. We paddled away from the land, and then he turned the boat to the north, following the line of the coast. It was a beautiful day, and it felt good to be out on the water.

'You are going to Alusi Krawain on business?' he asked as he rowed.

'More or less. I'm here for a research project, studying sculpture.'

He frowned. 'You must be very careful in Alusi Krawain,' he told me. 'It is very hot. A witch in the village paralysed my father. Back then, I was a teacher in a school, but I had to leave my job to care for my father.'

'Did you find out who the witch was?' I asked.

'I know who he was. I know him very well,' he said.

'But you haven't done anything about it?'

'We are afraid of such people,' he said. 'There is nothing we can do.'

As he was saying this, the wind started to blow. First it was a soft breeze, but then it stiffened, coming in stronger off the sea, stirring up the waves so that the water became choppy. I looked away from the land, towards the horizon. Grey rain clouds were racing towards us.

'A storm,' the boatman said, frowning just a little.

The wind grew stronger. The surface of the sea started to churn, making our little dugout buck and sway. Then the clouds caught up with us, and cold rain began to fall. The landmass of Yamdena to our west disappeared in a haze of greyness, and in only a few moments we were soaked. For the first time since coming to Indonesia, I remembered what it felt like to be truly, miserably cold. I hunched down in the bow of the boat, waiting for the storm to pass.

The wind continued to pick up strength. A heavy swell rose beneath us, and the dugout lurched. The boatman tried to turn the prow of the boat into the rising waves, so we were not side-on. The waves broke over the bow. I grabbed a plastic bucket from the bottom of the canoe and started to bail out water. The waves were becoming taller, and the wind was biting. Then the prow of the boat was wrenched upwards and the boatman fell backwards, almost letting slip his oar. He grabbed on to the sides of the dugout. For a moment I thought we were on the brink of capsize. It was then that I realised this seasoned sailor was afraid, and I felt a shudder of terror. The canoe was lifted by the high crest of a wave. It teetered for a moment, pointing towards the sky, then plummeted into the trough below. The strong current was tugging the boat side-on to the waves. The boatman kicked another oar towards me. I let go of the bucket and grabbed the oar, and together we turned the nose of the boat back into the next wave as it rose in front of us.

Then the rain started to ease, and the wind fell. The horizon cleared as the clouds receded away from us over the island. We could see land again – the villages of Lorwembun and Alusi Batjasi. Beneath us, the swell of the waves subsided. In a few more minutes, the sea had returned to a flat calm. The sun shone. Our clothes started to steam. I bailed out the last of the water. The boatman didn't meet my eye. He started to row again, steadily heading north up the coast. He seemed spooked. I thought it wise not to continue our conversation about witches.

Ⴟ

Not long afterwards a small bay opened up on the coastline. There was a cliff sheltering the bay, and steps leading to the village above.

'Alusi Krawain,' the boatman said. Then he lapsed back into silence.

By the time we were pulling the canoe up the secluded little beach, my shirt was almost dry. We tethered the boat on dry land, and the boatman turned to me. He took a deep breath, then he smiled.

'*Masih hidup*,' he said. 'Still alive.'

I followed him along the steep path that led up the hill to the village. When we reached the top of the hill the boatman asked for my letter. I handed it over. It was damp from the storm, but not irredeemably so. Then he strode into the village, indicating I should follow.

Near the open space at the heart of the village was a tree, and underneath the tree a number of people were sitting on a bamboo platform, sheltering from the heat of the late afternoon sun and chatting animatedly. They fell silent as we approached.

The boatman stopped, and read very slowly from the front of the letter, 'Ibu Lin and Bapak Rerebain?'

'That's me,' snapped a large and rather cross-looking woman in a white floral dress. 'I'm Ibu Lin. What do you want?' She glared at us mistrustfully through the thick lenses of her glasses. The boatman handed her the letter. Then, shaking my hand, he went off for whatever business it was that he was attending to in Alusi Krawain.

With the letter in hand, Ibu Lin heaved herself from the platform and strolled off up the street. When she had taken a few steps, she looked back over her shoulder and gave a curt nod to indicate that I was to follow. As I left, I heard the people gathered on the bamboo platform

— 86 —

discussing my arrival in the village: What was I doing there? Did I speak Indonesian? Where was I from? Why had I arrived with a letter for Ibu Lin?

My hostess led me into a house facing the village square, stooping as she passed through the door.

'Sit down,' she ordered when I had entered, pointing with a pudgy forefinger to a chair at the side of the room, and thrusting out her lower lip in a pout. She did not look the slightest bit happy to have me turning up on her doorstep. I began to question Suster Astrid's judgement.

I put down my bag, and sat down.

'You speak Indonesian?' she asked.

'Yes,' I said.

Ibu Lin flopped down into a chair opposite me. She pushed her glasses up her nose and, with a laboriously theatrical sigh, opened the letter. She read it through once, mouthing the words. By the time she had come to the end, her face had softened a little. Then Ibu Lin turned the letter over in her hand and started at the beginning again. She read it three times in all, glancing at me from time to time as she did so. I sat quietly, waiting for her to finish.

The walls of Ibu Lin's house were pasted with newspaper articles and photographs. Just above her shoulder was a photograph of John Major. The caption, in Indonesian, read: 'John Major, Britain's handsome Prime Minister'.

When at last she put the letter down and looked up at me, every trace of her former belligerence had evaporated, and tears were beading in the corners of her eyes. She shook her head, and took off her spectacles to dab them away. Placing her glasses back on her nose, she handed me the letter.

'May I read it?' I asked.

'Yes, read it,' she said.

It was a formal letter, asking that Ibu Lin and her husband Bapak

Rerebain look after me as best they were able while I stayed in Alusi Krawain. It mentioned their daughter, and made explicit reference to the debt of gratitude the Rerebains owed to Suster Astrid. When I handed the letter back, Ibu Lin smiled for the first time.

It was an extraordinary smile. Her jaw dropped and she drew back her lips to reveal gums that had receded through years of compulsive betel chewing, and an incomplete set of teeth, stained red. As she grinned at me, she rolled her eyes in a fashion that was at once both charming and terrifying. In both charm and terror, I was later to realise, Ibu Lin excelled.

She continued to beam at me, muttering, 'Good, good,' and looking me up and down. I smiled back stupidly. 'This is a letter from Suster Astrid,' she said, as if I did not know already. 'She says that you are here to study. She says that you are here for the pursuit of knowledge, to understand our lives here in Tanimbar, and that we should look after you.' Ibu Lin spread her palms and opened her eyes wide. 'And so you may stay here as long as you like. You will be as a son to us.' Ibu Lin leaned towards me, and patted me proprietarily on the arm. 'Of course,' she added, 'I will have to ask my husband. He makes all the decisions here. But he is bound to agree with me. He is a good man. He *always* agrees with me.'

I thanked her, and she excused herself to make tea. She returned with a glass of hot, sweet tea and a pile of sandwiches made from stale white bread, smeared with margarine and sprinkled with mounds of sugar.

'I have made you something to eat, as you are very thin,' she said. 'You must eat them all.'

I started to work my way through the sandwiches.

'Delicious?' she asked.

'Delicious,' I agreed. 'Very sweet.'

Ibu Lin smiled in satisfaction. 'You see,' she said, 'I know what Westerners like. I can make food for Westerners, not like the other people in this village. If you stayed with them, they would not know how to serve you. It is lucky you have come here.'

When I was finally done, she took the plate away.

Ibu Lin's husband came home later in the day. After his initial surprise at seeing me, as his wife had predicted, he did not voice any objections to my staying. Bapak Rerebain was a gentle man with a furrowed brow and a serious air. He lived, I guessed, somewhat in the shadow of his formidable wife. Ibu Lin spoke of him with a dismissive affection, saying repeatedly what a good husband he was, how he never disagreed with her. 'He does not even beat me,' she said, play-acting a husband beating his wife, her enormous arms flying. Bapak Rerebain smiled with embarrassment.

Ibu Lin and Bapak Rerebain made fine and generous hosts in Alusi Krawain. Thanks to their not inconsiderable kindness, I settled into the village quickly. For the first time since arriving in Tanimbar, I found myself having fun. Visitors came to the house to chat and joke. I felt relaxed and at ease. In the evenings – there being no electricity in Alusi Krawain, and thus no television or radio – people crowded into the house to see me, and Ibu Lin exhibited me with a fiercely protective pride. When anybody asked what she deemed to be too many questions, she snapped and growled at them.

'Leave him alone!' she said. 'Do you think he came half the way across the world just to answer your stupid questions?'

On the first evening that I was in Alusi Krawain, as we were sitting and chatting, with a group of villagers crowded into the house to watch, Ibu Lin – who knew a bit about anthropologists – asked if I had a cassette recorder with me.

I told her that I did. It was a small, portable, battery-operated machine that I had bought to record interviews. I had not yet used it.

'Bring it to me,' she said.

I went to fetch the cassette recorder. She studied it closely.

'Do you have any English music?' she said. I had only one cassette with anything on it, a taped copy of a Tom Waits album. Ibu Lin did not know who Tom Waits was, but she was keen to hear it. I took it out of my bag and inserted it into the cassette recorder. When I pressed play, Tom started to sing *Whistlin' Past the Graveyard*. And then, in front of an audience of astonished villagers, Ibu Lin started to dance. She strutted, rolled her eyes, swung her hips and gestured to me to join her.

Her husband gave a shy smile. 'Go on,' he said.

And so, there in Alusi Krawain – as Tom barked and yelped about Mean Mother Hubbard, about bloodhounds chasing the devil through the corn and about how he'd come to Baton Rouge to find himself a witch – Ibu Lin and I swaggered to and fro, and the people who had gathered to watch this peculiar spectacle laughed and clapped.

When we came to the end of the song, Ibu Lin insisted we go through the whole performance again. I pressed rewind, running the tape back, and once again pressed play. There in the hooligan night, Ibu Lin and I preened and prowled, singing along, whooping and rolling our eyes. We danced until we were exhausted, and the villagers clapped and stamped their feet. For the first time since coming to Tanimbar, I felt uncomplicated and at home.

9

WALUT

A couple of days after my arrival in the village, I was ready to go and meet Abraham – but the sculptor beat me to it, by coming to Ibu Lin and Bapak Rerebain's house to track me down. Bapak Rerebain ushered him inside. Ibu Lin did not get up to greet him. She just nodded at him, her mouth open, a bowl of betel nut on her lap.

Abraham was a thin, wiry man in his late fifties, with short-cropped grey hair. He looked physically strong and was dressed in a singlet and shorts, his feet bare. He had an animated air about him, and his face radiated forceful intelligence. But, I noted, he also looked desperately poor, his clothes old and tattered. He shook my hand firmly, and Bapak Rerebain indicated that he should sit down. Ibu Lin went to make tea, and we started to talk.

I told Abraham I had seen some of his sculptures in Saumlaki. He said that the sculptures his brother Pak Isak owned were of inferior quality, and that he was capable of producing far finer works. He had lived in Saumlaki with his brother several years ago, he said. Pak Isak was the younger of the two brothers. He had invited Abraham to the town to sculpt, saying he would work as his manager. But the business arrangement didn't suit either of them. Abraham was unhappy in Saumlaki and longed to return to the village, whilst Pak Isak found his brother hard to manage. There were disagreements about money. Pak Isak wanted Abraham to work harder, to produce more sculptures, to make sculptures that would sell. Abraham could not tolerate his art being subjected to such demands. He worked according to different dictates. So, after a few months, Abraham returned home to the village in frustration. The two brothers had not seen each other since.

There was bitterness in Abraham's voice as he told me the story, and I wondered how different Pak Isak's version of the tale might sound.

'It was too noisy in Saumlaki, anyway,' Abraham said. 'It was not possible to work with all that noise. But here I can work all I like. Here in Alusi Krawain it is calm and peaceful.'

'Are you still working?' I asked him.

'Sometimes,' he said, evasively. 'To be a sculptor, to be a great sculptor, you need patience. You need a calm and courageous heart. And you need to know the power of the wood. When people go into the forest to find wood, they see the large trees and they are afraid. The trees are sacred. The stones are sacred. Everything in the forest is sacred. That is what makes us afraid. If we wish to cut wood or to take stones to carve, we must pray to avert disaster, and then we must pray again before carving. This is how we respect the power of the wood.'

'And if you do not respect the power of the wood?'

Abraham frowned. 'Then you will make bad sculptures, and you will meet with misfortune.'

We continued to talk for a while, then Abraham got up to leave.

'Come to my house tomorrow,' he told me. 'We can talk more then.'

The following day, I went to Abraham's house. It was slightly downhill from where Ibu Lin and Bapak Rerebain lived, and was extremely spartan, even by Tanimbarese standards. Abraham invited me in, and he sat on a block of wood on the dirt floor. I sat on a rickety stool. Up in the rafters, geckos were calling to each other: *tok-ek, tok-ek*. Abraham was stripped to the waist, wearing only an old pair of stained shorts. A pair of spectacles sat low on his nose, set at a slight angle, the left arm broken.

'I have decided to make you a sculpture,' he said. 'I will make it for you as a gift.'

I had not expected this, and I felt wrong footed, unsure of the etiquette of the situation. 'Thank you,' I said.

Abraham cleared his throat. 'The other night,' he said, 'after I spoke to you, I returned home, and I found that my body was itching. Although I am sick, I knew that I had to make this sculpture for you. I will make it as a gift, so that you can take it back to Europe and prove my greatness to the people there.'

'That is very generous,' I said.

Abraham stopped me short. 'I am doing it because my body was itching. I am doing it because the ancestors want it. I am making the sculpture because of them. Do not say that I am generous.'

I hesitated. 'What will you make?'

'I will make you a *walut*,' he said

A *walut*, in Yamdenan, is an ancestor figurine. Before collectors and salesmen came to plunder Tanimbar's art to sell to museums and private collections in the West, *walut* were widespread. Kept above the *tavu* – the wooden house-altars that in the past stood at the centres of noble houses – these small sculptures condensed and concentrated the ritual heat of the ancestors. Even now in Tanimbar, long after the *tavu* were gone and genuine *walut* were few, people still treated those that remained with circumspection, even with fear.

Abraham pulled on his cigarette thoughtfully. A cloud of fragrant smoke formed in the shaft of afternoon light coming through the doorway. 'I will start tomorrow. I will go to cut wood, and I will start carving tomorrow.'

'How did you learn to sculpt?' I asked him.

'I didn't,' he said.

'You had no teacher?'

'No. Nobody taught me. I sculpt through the power of the *tetek nenek moyang*, through the power of the ancestors.'

Then Abraham told me the secret of his extraordinary talent. It started, he said, when he was at school. One day, his father – who was not a sculptor but instead a talented singer – took him into the forest. They walked for a long time, until Abraham no longer knew where they were. Then his father bent down and picked a leaf from a plant lying close to the forest floor. His father offered up prayers to the ancestors, and then gave his son the leaf to eat. It was bitter.

Abraham returned home with his father, the taste of the leaf in his mouth. That very same evening, without teacher or mentor or exemplar, he felt the itch to start carving in wood.

'My first sculpture,' he said, coughing through the clouds of clove cigarette smoke, 'was a figure of Sukarno. He was President back then. I made the most beautiful sculpture anybody had ever seen. I just let my heart follow the *tetek nenek moyang*, and I knew how to carve. The sculpture is now in a government building in the Kei Islands.'

Again, Abraham coughed, and I wondered what had happened to this bust in the years since Sukarno's fall from grace, after the coup that removed him from power back in 1965, and the bloodletting that followed. I wasn't sure whether Abraham was even aware that Sukarno was no longer President. His concerns seemed to exist on a different plane to this.

Abraham coughed a good long while, then he picked up the thread of the conversation again. 'But I cannot be arrogant,' he said. 'The power is not my own: it is my *kekuatan mata rumah*, the power of my household. It was passed from my father to me, and from his father to him. It isn't always carving. For my grandfather it was carving. For my father it was singing. For me it was carving. There is no way of telling what it will be. But this gift is also a burden: if I go without carving for a month, sometimes even a week, my body itches. I am uncomfortable. I cannot sit still. Smoking and palm-wine do not help. The itchiness becomes unbearable, and I have to start working.'

'Does working cure it?' I asked.

He threw his cigarette butt to one side. 'As soon as I go into the forest to cut wood, or I pick up my chisel,' he said, 'the itch goes, and I am at peace.' Then Abraham paused for a few moments so that he could cough fiercely into his hand. It was an unhealthy sounding cough.

'I will make you a *walut*,' he said when the coughing had died down, 'so you can take it back to the West and tell people about my gift.'

'Thank you,' I said. But Abraham, who didn't want thanks, because after all it was not his power, did not reply.

Ж

That evening, I headed back in the fading afternoon light, the sun setting over the forest to the west. A cool breeze was blowing in from the sea. It was possible to hear the distant suck of the waves against the coral. It was a beautiful evening. I sat down for a while and chatted with a small group of people gathered in the town square. Then I headed back to the Rerebains' house. Ibu Lin was sitting on her porch, watching people going past. Bapak Rerebain was pottering to and fro, doing small jobs around the house. Ibu Lin indicated that I should sit next to her. And as we sat, we talked about Abraham's *kekuatan mata rumah*.

The term literally means 'power of the eye of the house'. The 'eye of the house', or '*mata rumah*', is a term for the extended household, understood through the paternal line. It was a common concept across Maluku. The term '*mata*', although literally meaning 'eye', has a meta-phorical sense, suggesting a point of importance or centrality; a pivot point or point of origin. Thus *mata air*, or 'eye of water', means 'spring';

matahari, or 'eye of the days', means 'sun'; *mata kaki*, or 'eye of the foot', means 'ankle'; and *mata pencarian*, or 'eye of the livelihood', means one's main income. The eye of the house, then, is not so much the household as it is the set of kinship relations around which the household pivots, the origin point and the nucleus of the household.

When I told her about Abraham's *kekuatan mata rumah*, Ibu Lin – who made it her business not to be impressed by her neighbours – was less than awed. To be sure, Abraham was skilled in working wood, she said. But powers such as his were common in Tanimbar. Different households, different *mata rumah*, had their own powers. Such powers were usually associated with a root or a leaf that was considered to be filled with ritual heat, but the ultimate source of the power was not the root or the leaf, but instead the ancestors themselves.

Ibu Lin popped a bit more betel nut in her mouth, and glared at me. 'I have my own *kekuatan mata rumah*,' she said, jabbing a finger towards her sizeable bosom.

'You do?'

'Of course,' she said. I should not have been surprised: Ibu Lin did not seem to me to be a woman who was lacking in power.

Ibu Lin told me that the plant associated with her power was a tall flowering grass, the root of which, when ground up, could be efficacious in a number of ways. When the grass blossomed, it broke out in clusters of small white flowers with brownish hearts, and these flowers were much favoured by butterflies.

'People come to me,' she said, 'like butterflies do to that flower. I am very attractive.'

At this point, Bapak Rerebain, who had been hovering in the background, came and joined us. 'When I was young,' he interjected, putting up a seat, 'she was the most popular girl in the village. All the young men wanted to marry her.' I detected a hint of wistfulness in his voice.

Ibu Lin continued. 'It is my *mata rumah*, not Bapak's. He does not have this power. But I do. Let me give you proof of my attractiveness. Watch!'

Then she cast her eye down the main street of the village from the shade of her porch. There was a figure in the distance, walking down the road. Ibu Lin slumped back in her chair with exaggerated nonchalance, and stuffed some more betel nut into her mouth. She chewed, pretending to be deep in thought.

Bapak Rerebain nodded at me conspiratorially, and echoed his wife's words in a hushed voice. 'Watch! Here is proof.'

As the figure approached, Ibu Lin glanced sideways at me. Then she looked heavenwards again with a sigh. The figure, a man in his early thirties, drew closer.

'Good afternoon, Ibu Lin,' he called out as he came within range, and gave a little wave. It was all very cordial.

Ibu Lin affected surprise. 'Good afternoon,' she replied, a note of triumph in her voice.

When the man had disappeared into the distance again, she swung round in her chair to face me. 'Did you see that?' she asked.

'I saw him say hello,' I said.

'Did you hear him call out?'

'I heard him say good afternoon, yes.'

'Exactly!' She slapped the arm of her chair, and smiled her terrifying smile. 'Exactly! *Everyone* who passes by calls out to me. That is my *kekuatan mata rumah*. People are attracted to me as butterflies to a flower. They didn't call out to you or to Bapak Rerebain. They called out to *me*.'

'Oh,' I said. I was not sure what else to say.

'It is no coincidence,' she went on, mustering her proofs, 'that when you came to Alusi Krawain you came straight to me. Tell me, did you speak to anyone in the village before me?'

'No, but Suster Astrid gave me a letter...'

'Suster Astrid? It was nothing to do with Suster Astrid! She only sent you to me because of the power of the root. My root is hot. It has a lot of power. Whenever anyone comes to the village, because of the power of my root, it is me they come to.'

The power of Ibu Lin's root was a matter of considerable personal pride. Over the days that followed, Ibu Lin continued to tell me about the many ways in which it could be efficacious. A little of the root ground up and slipped into someone's coffee, food or cigarette, she said, was effective in calming their anger, although only if it was used in this way by Ibu Lin herself. And, she assured me, if she gave me some to put in my pocket when I left Alusi Krawain, women would come flocking around me like butterflies, such that no mortal woman would be able to resist my charms.

'I will give you some of my root,' she pressed me eagerly, 'and then you will see. Then you will have no problem finding a wife. This is *adat*.'

The following afternoon, as I was making my way along the main street to Abraham's house, a figure approached me. He was a youngish man, stockily built and not yet thirty, and he was staggering and lurching. He didn't look drunk so much as *strange*. He had his head down and was staring at the road. I stepped to one side to let him pass, and at that moment I realised that something was not right. He looked up and met my eyes, and I saw there was a terrifying blank anger to his gaze. He stooped and thrust his head forward, then he clenched his fists and let out a horrible screech, the veins in his forehead and neck standing out, his eyes bulging. I stopped and faced him. We stood like that for a few moments, our noses no more than a foot away from each other. I glanced down to his clenching and unclenching fists, and was relieved to see he didn't have a knife.

I carefully took a step back. 'Good afternoon,' I said.

He did not reply, but at that moment he seemed to become confused. I looked into his eyes, and saw something hollow in his expression, as if the man who had inhabited his body had some time since departed. We stood like this a few moments more, staring at each other. Then, with a gurgling sound made at the back of his throat, he stepped to one side and walked off down the street, shouting oaths and shaking his fists. I watched him go.

I was about to go on my way when I looked to the side of the road. There, in the shade of a tree, was an old man, shaking with silent laughter. I glared at him, and in reply he lifted his hand in greeting and cheerfully beckoned me over. I went and joined him.

'What was wrong with him?' I asked, pointing to the figure disappearing down the road.

'He is mad,' the old man said. He put his finger to his brow at an angle, to indicate that he thought the other man's brains were not set at quite the right angle. 'Mad. Crazy, you know?'

'Yes,' I said.

'But it is his own fault,' the old man said.

'His own fault? Why?'

'His family did a stupid thing. You must not feel sorry for him. He received the punishment he deserved.'

'Who punished him?' I asked.

I should have known the answer. 'The *tetek nenek moyang*,' he said. The ancestors.

The story that the old man told me was, more or less, like this. Several years before, my assailant had been a gifted student. He had been studying at the University of Pattimura in Ambon to be a teacher. He lived in the house of his uncle with his brother and sisters, all of whom were also studying to become teachers. But it was expensive to send so many children to university, and so, back home in Alusi Krawain, their parents struggled to make ends meet. Money was short, and although they had some financial help from relations, the bills were mounting up. It seemed fortuitous, then, when a small group of Westerners came to Alusi Krawain in search of *barang antik*, or antiques. The family members, desperate for money, negotiated a price for the heirloom gold that they held in their family. The Westerners paid in dollars – cold, hard cash – then they left the village, their suitcases full of antiques. They were never seen again.

This was a mistake. Heirloom gold is not a personal possession to be bought and sold at will. It is instead something to be exchanged between households. The Tanimbar Islands were criss-crossed by a network of invisible threads, pathways that represented affiliations between households, channels for the flow of heirloom goods: gold earrings called *loran* and *kmena*, pendants and necklaces, elephant tusks and shell armbands, swords and ikat cloths. Like the *kula* ring in the Trobriand Islands – made famous by the Polish anthropologist Bronisław Malinowski – these exchange pathways cemented alliances between households and villages as goods flowed from noble household to noble household, from *mata rumah* to *mata rumah*. But as the twentieth century had worn on, this vast, ever-turning network of exchange pathways had become increasingly ragged and patchy, the flow of heirloom gold ever more erratic. Hard-up households pressed by hunger, poverty or greed increasingly risked the wrath of both their forebears and their contemporaries by selling off heirloom gold. As a result, relations between households had become strained, and the fabric that wove together alliances had grown increasingly threadbare.

The ancestors did not take kindly to this diminution of their power. It was a dangerous thing to sell off heirloom gold. And so, a few days after the valuables had been handed over, after the foreigners had left, the family in Alusi Krawain received a letter from Ambon, written in the hand of the uncle. The children, the uncle said, had all fallen ill with a strange affliction. All four of them – overnight, and quite innocent of what had occurred back in their home village – had been struck by a curious madness. The best doctors in Ambon had been called, but no cause for the illness could be found.

Three of the children subsequently recovered as mysteriously as they had first succumbed. They were able to resume their studies, and were now elsewhere in the archipelago, carrying out their vocations as teachers. The eldest son, however, never recovered. He was sent home, to be looked after back in the village.

All this happened five years ago, the old man said, and still the young man was sick. The family's only consolation was the thought that perhaps the foreigners who had made off with the heirloom gold had suffered a similarly terrible fate, through shipwreck or plane crash or disease.

By the time the old man had finished explaining all this, the young man had long gone, and I realised I was late for my appointment with Abraham. So I continued on my way to Abraham's house, turning off the main street and picking my way along the track down the hill.

I knocked on the door.

'Come in!' Abraham coughed.

I could smell the scent of clove cigarettes. Inside, I found the sculptor with a machete in one hand and a piece of ironwood between his bare, dusty feet. He was hard at work on a new sculpture.

10

BUFFALO KILLER

Abraham looked up and smiled. 'See! I have already started work,' he said. 'Come in!' He put the machete down and stretched his limbs.

I sat down on the low stool by the wall. Abraham had been working for a while. He looked like he needed a rest.

We chatted, and a few passers-by drifted into the house to smoke and watch our conversations. Abraham took up his machete again and continued shearing off wedges of wood with an ease that suggested years of practice. Abraham's wife came out of the back room to cast her eye over the scene. She flashed me a smile, and retired again into the darkness.

After an hour or so, Abraham put down his tools and looked up.

'I need a rest,' he said, pointing to his chest. His breath was slightly strained. He put his hand out for a cigarette, and one of the guests handed him one. As he inhaled, he coughed again. The cough sounded heavy on his chest. 'This wood is very hard. It is not easy to carve,' he said by way of explanation. 'Smoking is good. It relaxes the chest.'

'You seem very skilled,' I said.

Abraham picked up the machete and ran his thumb along the blade approvingly. 'It is a little blunt today,' he said, deflecting my praise, 'but it is a good machete.' He held it up so that he could see the blade glint a little in the light. 'You know,' he said, 'once I killed a sleeping buffalo with this machete.'

The spectators all murmured in approval.

'You did?' I said.

Abraham did not smile. 'It was a big buffalo,' he said, 'asleep in the forest. I crept up on it, kept downwind. Then, when I was close enough, I lifted my machete' – he held the handle of the machete in both hands, and lifted it above his head, the tendons in his neck tautening, a hunter's intensity in his eyes – 'and brought it down on the buffalo's neck. *Chop*!'

He swung the machete. The men smoking in the darkness laughed. Despite myself, I flinched. A ripple of laughter went round the room. Abraham grinned.

'Do you still hunt?' I asked.

He shook his head. 'Not now. I am too old and sick. To hunt buffalo you need to be young and strong.' Then Abraham sighed, and returned to work on the figure. 'Once,' he said, 'I could kill a buffalo with this machete, and now I hardly have the strength to make a small sculpture.'

'How do you know where to cut?' I asked him.

'If you have a calm heart, and you know the power of the wood, then you know where to cut. The figure is already there, inside the wood. If you listen to the wood, you can bring the figure to life. You must know the power of the wood.'

I thought of Michelangelo: 'In every block of marble I see a statue as plain as though it stood before me... I have only to hew away the rough walls that imprison the lovely apparition to reveal it to the other eyes as mine see it.' Outside, the light was fading. Abraham seemed to be becoming tired.

After another half hour or so, he put down the machete. 'I am finished for the day,' he said. 'Come back tomorrow to have a look at the progress of my work.' His voice was rough, and his chest sounded tight. 'I need to rest,' he said.

Then he lit another cigarette to ease his breathing.

𐌗

Over the following few days, the sculpture began to take shape. Out of the wood – as if it had been there all along, just as Abraham had said – emerged the figure of the *walut*. After three or four days, the rough form of the little figure was completed. Cut with assurance from the wood, it was dressed in a loincloth and headcloth, sitting cross-legged on a platform. In its hands the figure held up a bowl, and around its arms were armbands. The eyes were closed as if in rapt concentration, and a pendant – the head of a buffalo – hung around the figure's neck.

'The figure I am carving is a *sori luri*,' Abraham told me.

The anthropologist Susan McKinnon explains that *sori luri*, which can be translated as 'the bows of the boat', was traditionally the term for an official who took the lead in village rituals. Standing as if at the bows of the stone boat that was the village, the *sori luri* was the first to speak at gatherings of the community, the one responsible for haruspication and the reading of omens.

Abraham told me how, when the people of the village were about to set forth beyond the village walls and fortifications, the *sori luri* would read signs in the guts of chickens to tell of the success or failure of the coming enterprise. The bowl that the little sculpted figure held, Abraham explained, contained the entrails. In times of war there was an exact correlation between the length of the entrails of the sacrificed chicken and the number of warriors who would be killed in battle. That was how things were in those days, Abraham said, in the time of the ancestors.

As Abraham carved, I commented on the skill with which he was working – by this time he was using a small penknife rather than his buffalo-slaying machete. He brushed my compliment brusquely to one side. I said again that I admired his skill, that the work he was producing was very impressive.

Abraham stopped carving. 'It is still crude,' he said. 'There is much work to be done.'

'But still,' I persisted, 'it is a very fine sculpture.'

A look of anger passed over Abraham's face. 'Do not praise my work,' he said. 'It is not on account of my own skill. It is because of the power of my household that I can carve. My skill comes from the ancestors. If people praise my work, there is a danger that I might become conceited. Then the ancestors will be angry.'

'But the ancestors – '

Abraham held up his penknife and silenced me with a fierce look. 'Be careful what you say about the ancestors,' he muttered. 'You are from England. You may not believe in their power, but you must be careful. They are listening to us all the time. Even now they are listening to our conversation. They do not easily forget.'

I apologised, and was relieved to see that Abraham took my apology in good heart. What the ancestors thought of my clumsiness I do not know. Abraham returned to his work.

'It is all right,' he said at length. 'You do not understand our ways here. Things are very different in Tanimbar from the way they are in England. You do not understand *adat*.'

I watched him as he continued to coax the little *sori luri* from the block of ironwood.

That night, I sat outside the house with Ibu Lin and Bapak Rerebain, enjoying the night air. Ibu Lin was pleased that things were going well with Abraham, and she was on expansive form. She asked about my family back home, about what I intended to do in the future, about why it was I had chosen to come to Tanimbar.

But then she became quiet and melancholy. She patted me on the arm. 'I am pleased you came to me,' she said. 'Bapak and I had a son, but he died several years ago. He got sick and he died.'

I wasn't sure what to say, so I said nothing and let Ibu Lin go on talking.

'He would be your age now, more or less,' she said. 'We were sad when he died because God took our son from us. But when you arrived in Alusi Krawain with Suster Astrid's letter, and when you came straight to my house, I knew that God had given me a new son.'

I smiled at her awkwardly. This unexpected adoption was humbling, but it made me ill at ease. As a son, I suspected, I would inevitably disappoint her.

As we were talking, a dark column of smoke began to rise from the forests to the south. People came out of their houses and gathered in the village square.

Ibu Lin touched my arm lightly. 'Wait,' she said.

The smoke was dark against the blue-black evening sky. I could hear people debating in Yamdenan. Ibu Lin got to her feet.

'What is happening?' I asked her.

'People from Alusi Krawain are burning the fields of the people from Kalaan,' she said.

'Why?'

'The Kalaan people build plantations on our territory, so we are burning them down. It will teach them a lesson.'

We watched the smoke rise. 'If I wake you up in the night,' Ibu Lin said, 'you must be prepared to run. The people from Kalaan may come to the village for revenge. If you hear the alarm, get out of bed and run as fast as you can.'

'Where should I run?' I asked her.

'Into the forest. All the way to Meyano Bab if you must. Anywhere but towards the south or down to the beach. The people from Kalaan are fierce. We do not want you to be killed.'

Ibu Lin was not joking. I nodded slowly. 'Does this kind of thing happen often?' I asked her.

'Most years, yes,' she said. 'Come, let's go inside.'

Throughout the nineteenth century, inter-village warfare was common in Tanimbar. In the twentieth century these territorial disputes sub-sided, but they didn't entirely disappear. Occasionally violence flared, and sometimes lives were lost. Fortunately, however, the skirmish on the borders of Alusi Krawain turned out to be no more than that. The evening was tense, and I slept uneasily, but the night passed peacefully enough. There were no alarms, no raging fires of retribution, no hordes with machetes hunting people down on the beaches. The next day, the sun came up on a village at peace. I heard no more of the dispute with the people from Kalaan. I ate breakfast contentedly in the company of the family dog, Roki. Ibu Lin had taken to feeding me eggs in large quantities, in the unshakeable conviction that Westerners had a passion for them. Every mealtime, she fed me at least three: boiled, fried, scrambled, made into little omelettes or added to vegetables. I tried to persuade her that, whilst I liked eggs, my enthusiasm for them had limits. But Ibu Lin would hear nothing of it.

'Of course you must have eggs,' she said to me. 'You come all this way to Alusi Krawain, and you think I cannot afford to give you eggs.'

Roki and I had something of a conspiratorial relationship. I liked Roki. I spoke dog better than I spoke Indonesian, and he made few demands upon me. He liked me in return, because when Ibu Lin was out of sight I would often slip him an egg or two, in an attempt to drive my daily total down from nine or ten to a more reasonable five or six. This went on until one day Ibu Lin found Roki going at a boiled egg under the table – I had underestimated how long she would be out of the room – and I had to dissimulate rapidly and tell her, not very convincingly, that the egg had rolled off the plate.

'Bad dog,' she said. Roki looked at me accusingly.

After breakfast, I took a walk up to the Catholic church in the village. Most villages in Tanimbar have imposing churches that are aligned, according to traditional custom, not east to west, but with the altar at the landward end and the door at the seaward end. Abraham had told me that he had made a sculpture to hang in the church, a crucifixion. It was not a 'traditional' sculpture like that of the *sori luri*, he said, but many people praised it.

The church door was open, and inside the building had a musty, cobwebbed air. I walked towards the altar and looked up to see Abraham's crucifixion, pale skinned and beautifully fashioned, larger than life-size. I took a photograph, stood there in the dark for a while and then went down to speak with Abraham at his house.

He was seated on the floor, working with ever more intense care on the sculpture, frowning with concentration as he pared the wood with his penknife. I took a seat and watched him work. Abraham's tools were few: a machete for roughing out the sculpture, a cheap penknife for the finer work and, in place of a file, a piece of hardwood around which he had pinned a rough fish skin that was as abrasive as any metal file. Despite the unpromising tools that in other hands would have made careful work impossible, Abraham worked with astonishing skill. It was awe-inspiring to watch him. He did not make a single false move.

'I saw your crucifixion in the Church,' I said.

'Ah,' he said, and then paused. I was hesitant about praising the sculpture, not wanting to draw his anger again. 'I am not a Christian,' he said to me. 'I am a Muslim.'

'Oh,' I said.

Abraham started to cough. He lit a cigarette. 'I am glad you have seen the sculpture,' he said. 'But this is more important.' He pointed to the *sori luri*. Then he went back to work.

It was fascinating watching Abraham. When his work demanded full attention, he was silent, his expression serious. But at other times he was relaxed, his movements fluid, and he chatted about his art, about the past and about the ancestors. Occasionally he stopped to smoke a cigarette and to cough alarmingly.

Whilst carefully filing down the wood with his fish-skin file, Abraham looked up at me and said, 'This sculpture is hot.'

'Hot?' I asked him.

'Yes. It is a *walut*. It has been made thanks to the ancestors' gift, so it is hot.'

He continued filing and, although he had stopped speaking, I said nothing. I sensed that he had more to say. He paused and coughed again. 'That is why I have made it as a gift for you. My talent is a gift from the ancestors, and I make the sculpture as a gift.' He glanced up at me.

'Thank you,' I said.

'It is not something to buy and sell,' he said. 'It is a gift.'

'Yes,' I said. 'I understand.'

'But it would be dangerous for you to take it home like this,' he went on. 'It would be bad *adat*. We must have a *mandi adat*, to cool the sculpture.'

I thought of the young man whose family had sold off the household's heirloom gold, and I asked him, 'What would happen if I took it now, if we didn't have any *mandi adat*?'

Abraham raised his eyebrows, then put down his file and sighed. He pushed his spectacles up his nose. 'I don't know,' he said. 'But I do know this: there was one man in Alusi Krawain who sold a sculpture to a Westerner. When the buyer arrived back in America, he opened the box, and the sculpture was gone.'

'The man from Alusi Krawain cheated him?'

'No, the man was honest. It was the ancestors. They did not want the sculpture to go. So the American got home and found the sculpture had gone. Then, a few weeks later, the sculpture reappeared in the owner's plantation here in Tanimbar, as he was digging in the soil. It had come all the way home. These things happen here in Tanimbar. You may not believe these things, with your science and your knowledge, but we Tanimbarese people see these things with our own eyes and so we believe. If you take the sculpture away without a *mandi adat*, it could be dangerous. Your plane could crash on the way home, or you could get sick, because the sculpture is still hot. I do not want you to risk these dangers, so we must have a *mandi adat*. The *mandi adat* will make the sculpture cool. Ask Ibu Lin. She will know. It is better for you if you do all of this according to *adat*, so you do not suffer later.'

X

I arrived back at Ibu Lin and Bapak Rerebain's house towards sunset, and there I asked them about the *mandi adat*. They both nodded seriously.

'Yes,' Bapak Rerebain said softly, 'this is good. It is wise to have a *mandi adat*.'

Over dinner, Bapak Rerebain explained what was involved. After the sculpture was finished, he said, we would go to Abraham's house. I should bring a bottle of palm-wine and a small sum of money to act as a 'cork'. I knew from reading Drabbe and McKinnon that in *adat* ritual transactions in Tanimbar, offerings of palm-wine had to be accompanied by a cork consisting of either a small sum of money or else some gold earrings. In addition, Bapak Rerebain said, Ibu Lin would contribute heirloom gold to exchange – a pair of *loran* earrings – so that the *adat* would be heavy.

'You will give Abraham some gold on my behalf?' I was taken aback by this act of generosity.

Bapak Rerebain nodded. 'That is normal here. You are a member of our household. You are our son. If we in our household want to perform *adat*, we must give gold to make the *adat* heavy. If the *adat* is not heavy enough, then you will come to harm. If we give you some *loran* to exchange for Abraham's gift, you will not have any difficulties.'

When Bapak offered to contribute heirloom gold, I realised Abraham's gift was a more complex and weighty thing than I could have imagined. As the French anthropologist Marcel Mauss pointed out, there is a difference between the exchange of gifts and the exchange of commodities. When I go into the *boulangerie* to buy a croissant, I go my own way without a further thought given to the baker; but when I exchange gifts, I am drawn into a more abiding set of relationships and mutual obligations – because a gift, for Mauss, is never free. As an honorary son of the Rerebain household, I realised that I was now up to my neck in a system of exchange the mechanics of which I could not hope to comprehend, implicated in a web of obligations and intersecting forces of which I had little understanding. And, in my own entanglement, I had also caught Ibu Lin and Bapak Rerebain in this same web.

The *mandi adat* would begin, Bapak Rerebain explained, with my offering the palm-wine to Abraham. Then prayers would be made to the ancestors and the palm-wine sprinkled.

'When the *mandi adat* takes place,' he said, his forehead furrowing, 'you must say nothing at all. I will take care of everything. It is important that you do not speak.'

I nodded.

'We will ask the ancestors to approve the exchange,' he said. 'They will answer us using the voices of the *tokek*' – the large lizards that rummage through the rafters of houses in Tanimbar for insects and spiders to eat – 'and only if the *tetek nenek moyang* agree can the exchange can take place.'

'The ancestors will speak through the mouths of lizards?'

Bapak Rerebain smiled. 'You will only hear the lizards' voices, because you do not know *adat*, but we people who know *adat* will hear the ancestors when the lizards speak.'

'And if they do not agree?'

He smiled. 'They will agree. This is good *adat*, so they will agree.'

A *walut* in exchange for heirloom gold; heat for heat – this was gift giving, not commerce. Cementing relationships between households, but with the added complication of me – an outsider, an *orang bule* – somewhere in the middle.

Once exchanged, Bapak Rerebain went on, the *walut* would be washed clean of ritual heat. It would simply be a sculpture, a block of wood, no longer hot, no longer dangerous. And I would head home, to show my fellow countrymen the pinnacle of Abraham's art.

Bapak Rerebain leant forward. 'There is one final stage,' he said. 'After the exchange, Abraham will ask for money, as a sign of your gratitude.'

'How much?' I said.

Bapak shrugged 'How can I tell you? It is a gift.'

'How much, roughly, would you say is enough?' I pressed.

'That is your decision. I cannot tell you that. You are not buying the sculpture, you are giving a gift, so do not give Abraham too much. But do not give him too little, because that will look mean.'

'How about enough for a couple of sacks of rice?' I suggested.

Phrased this way, Bapak Rerebain was prepared to cautiously agree that this might be sufficient. 'Yes. In Tanimbar, one could give him a couple of sacks of rice. That would probably satisfy him.'

'And if Abraham is not satisfied?'

'He will ask for more, but you need not feel obliged to give it to him. A gift, after all, is a gift.'

Ibu Lin looked fierce. 'Do not be too generous,' she said, spitting out a jet of red betel-juice onto the dusty road.

11

OCTOPUS

It turned out, however, that the *mandi adat* had to be postponed, because during the days that followed I had other things on my mind.

Early the following morning, long before dawn, I woke with pains in my stomach. My head swirled with feverish images. When I closed my eyes, I could hear a strange humming inside my head. Outside, the village was silent. I lay awake waiting for the pain to subside, but instead it became stronger. There was a sharp jabbing in my stomach, accompanied by a background pulsing throb. It was a hot night, and I had been sweating in my sleep. My sheets stank of sweat and of illness.

I need a shit, I thought.

Very slowly, I swung my legs over the side of the bed and sat up. I was dizzy, and sitting up was hard work. I woozily slipped on my shoes, and swayed, not certain I could stand upright. Holding onto the doorpost, I eased myself to my feet and crept out of the room as quietly as I could, so as not to wake Ibu Lin and Bapak Rerebain, who were sleeping next door. I fumbled with the front door and stepped out into the deserted street.

The moon was fat in the sky, lighting up the road so the houses and trees cast dark shadows. Shivering in the soft night breeze, I held my stomach, a tightly knotted ball. Then I made my way down the road, stepping over the sleeping forms of hunting dogs. Coming to the corner of the street, I took the path that led along a low ridge behind the backs of the houses, and opened the door of the little thatched toilet. I fumbled for matches and lit a candle. I squatted down. My bowels gave way, and there was a terrible stench of shit and fever.

On the wall was a huge centipede, glinting yellow and malign in the candlelight. I watched it make its way up to the grass roof where it disappeared. I was circumspect towards centipedes. I didn't trust them. They had painful bites, and purposes that were beyond my comprehending.

I squatted there for a long time, until my bowels were empty. Then I washed myself clean, and stood up. The pain had subsided a little. I decided to make my way back to bed.

When I stepped back out of the latrine into the street, the cold air made me shiver. I felt sick. I started to lurch back up the path and onto the main street, towards the house. Then, about twenty yards from Ibu Lin and Bapak Rerebain's house, I made a mistake. What I took to be a shadow in the road was instead a sleeping hunting dog. It slid from under me with a yelp, abruptly awakened from dreams of the hunt. Then the dog rounded on me, crouching low, drawing back its lips to reveal two rows of pointed teeth. I backed off. The dog began to bark. Its barking woke the others, and in a moment every dog in the village was awake, and a pack of snarling, snapping hounds clustered around me. I aimed a kick at one of the fiercest dogs – it retreated with a pitiful whine – then I ran towards the house and slammed the door behind me. Outside I heard yelps of frustration. I collapsed on the bed, my heart thudding in my chest. Outside, the dogs lay down in the road and began to bay and howl. The dull ache in my stomach returned. I looked at my watch. It was four o' clock in the morning.

𐌗

When they discovered me on my sickbed the following morning, Ibu Lin and Bapak Rerebain were concerned. Bapak Rerebain said he would accompany me to the village clinic, so that I could be treated for my illness.

Later that morning, having sent a messenger down to tell Abraham that I would not be able to come and see him as planned, Bapak Rerebain led me up the hill to a small, neat building on the edge of the village. There was a well-tended fenced garden outside, with a sculpture of Our Lady of Fatima on a plinth. The Virgin gazed towards the heavens with a look of bored piety. Bapak Rerebain knocked on the door of the clinic. There did not seem to be anyone about. He knocked again. Eventually a tiny, wizened little nun appeared, dressed in immaculately starched white.

She gave me a gappy smile. '*Selamat datang*!' she said. *Welcome*. Then she led us into her consultancy room.

The room was small and dingy, without much light. Unlabelled bottles of potion were lined up on the shelves. The nun sat opposite me, swinging her legs.

'Poor thing,' she said reflectively. Then she beamed at me with a look of undiluted kindness.

I smiled back feebly.

The nun turned to Bapak Rerebain. 'Is he ill?' she asked.

'He is,' said Bapak Rerebain. I let him answer for me. I didn't have much appetite for conversation. In fact, I didn't have much appetite for anything at all.

'What's wrong with him?'

Bapak Rerebain indicated I should speak. 'My stomach,' I said.

The little nun's face lit up. 'He speaks Indonesian!' she exclaimed, delighted. She turned to me. 'So, you have a bad stomach?'

'Yes,' I said.

'He also has a fever,' Bapak Rerebain added.

'Are you dizzy?'

I nodded. The nun put her hand to my forehead. From the expression of worry on his face, it looked as if Bapak Rerebain did not believe I would last until sunset. The nun took my wrist, feeling for a pulse. She appeared satisfied.

'I have medicine for you,' she said. 'It will make you well.'

I smiled in thanks. The nun reached up to the shelf and ran her finger along the line of jars. She selected a bottle of murky blue potion plugged with a grubby cork, and placed it on the table. Then she took down a rusting Golden Virginia tobacco tin.

'This will make you better,' she said. Her smile was sweet and artless.

She prised the lid off the tin. Inside, lying on a bed of cotton wool, was a syringe. She carefully removed the syringe from the tin and began to fill it with the blue liquid.

Bapak Rerebain smiled reassuringly at me. 'She has very good medicine here,' he said. 'It will make you better.'

My mind was working slowly. It took me a few moments to realise what was happening. I thought about HIV. I thought about hepatitis. I thought about God-knows-what kind of blood-borne diseases.

'No,' I mumbled, 'no injections.'

The nun pretended not to hear. She withdrew the syringe from the bottle and squirted a bit of potion into the air, a blue arc. Then she looked at the needle with every appearance of satisfaction.

'Roll up your sleeve,' she said.

'No,' I said.

The nun looked surprised. 'You are afraid?'

I did not reply.

'It is only a very small needle,' she said. 'There's no need to be afraid.'

Bapak Rerebain turned to face me. My obstinacy brought out a paternal sternness I had not seen in him before.

'It would be better for you if you let her inject you,' he said. 'Then you will be cured. It is only one small injection.'

'No,' I said. 'The needle is not clean.'

The little nun paused. Then she opened a drawer and rummaged for a while. She took out some fresh cotton wool and she wiped the needle with care. 'There,' she said. 'It's clean.'

'No,' I said again. 'No injections.'

The nun's hand hovered, clutching the syringe as she tried to judge whether I would change my mind. Then she put the syringe down on the table and sighed. 'If you do not wish to be injected,' she said sadly, 'I cannot inject you.'

The nun squirted the blue liquid back into the bottle and corked it again. Wiping off the syringe, she returned it to the sterile environment of the Golden Virginia tobacco tin, and placed the tin back on the shelf to await a more co-operative patient. Ferreting around in her drawer for a while longer, she found some pills: four black, four white and four yellow. She put them in twists of brown paper.

'These are not as good as injections, but they might make you better.'

I went home with Bapak Rerebain and took the pills as instructed. But by the following day, my condition had worsened. And when after three more days I still showed no signs of recovering, the Rerebains were becoming very worried indeed. Most of the time I slept, lost in tangled fever-dreams. In moments of lucidity, I wondered how Abraham was and how the sculpture was progressing – but I hardly had energy to struggle to the latrine, let alone to go and speak with Abraham.

The nun's remedies having failed, Ibu Lin and her husband convened a council of villagers to discuss my illness. When they had gathered – around fifteen people in all, both men and women – I was summoned from my room. I was weak and had barely eaten for the previous few days. I came out of my room to see chairs arranged around the walls of the front room, and fifteen stern, worried faces.

'*Selamat pagi*,' I said. *Good morning*. But I was not sure whether it was morning or afternoon. I didn't even know what day of the week it was.

A wave of giddiness and nausea rose over me. Bapak Rerebain gently led me to a chair. I sat down, listening to the men tutting and the women making clucking maternal noises.

'Poor thing,' one woman said in Indonesian. 'He is so far from home.'

I looked at the gathered company. In the centre of the row of chairs facing me was a toothless old man, his skin stretched taut over a skeletal frame. He had an air of authority, and people seemed to be deferring to him. There was an inner tension to him that made him somehow rather frightening. He glanced around the room, flexing his long, bare toes. Once I was seated, the old man spoke. His voice was high pitched and slightly wheezing. He spoke in Yamdenan, and I had no idea what he was saying – but the more he spoke, the more animated he became. By the end he was waving his arms around, pointing at me repeatedly, pressing home rhetorical questions with emphatic, almost hysterical cadences. When he eventually drew to a close there was silence.

I wanted to go to the latrine. I wanted to go to sleep. I wanted to be anywhere but there, in that room, with the frightening old man with his high-pitched voice, and the committee of village elders gathered to discuss my fate.

Then Bapak Rerebain began to speak, still in Yamdenan, and a wave of murmuring approval passed around the room. One of the women spoke next. Then the old man again. I closed my eyes and waited for the discussion to come to an end. Eventually there was silence. All eyes in the room turned to me. Bapak Rerebain shifted in his seat with unease.

'It is like this,' he said, his voice apologetic, his shoulders drooping a little. 'The other day, when you went to talk to Abraham, did you pass the house of an old man?'

I shrugged. I was having difficulty in concentrating. I wondered if I was going to be sick.

'You must think,' Bapak Rerebain said. 'Did you pass the house of an old man?'

'Maybe,' I replied. 'I don't know. I passed lots of houses.'

'He lives down the hill,' Bapak Rerebain prompted helpfully.

'The house made of split bamboo,' added someone else, by way of explanation. 'Did you pass that house?'

'I don't know.' There were plenty of old men in Alusi Krawain. There were plenty of houses made of split bamboo.

Bapak Rerebain smiled. 'He is confused,' he said. There were murmurs of agreement.

'You must have passed his house,' said Bapak Rerebain. 'It's on the way as you go north from here.'

'Then I suppose I did.'

There were more mutterings from the crowd.

'Did the old man give you anything?' Bapak Rerebain pressed.

I wanted to go back to bed and sleep off the sickness. 'I don't know,' I said. 'I really don't know.'

'Did he give you anything to eat or drink?'

'No.' I shook my head. 'Nobody gave me anything to eat or drink.' The nausea was worse now.

'*Tuan*!' Bapak Rerebain's voice took on an unusually commanding tone. 'This is very important. You must try hard to answer our questions. Did the old man say anything to you? Did he say anything like, "Oh, you have such beautiful white skin"?'

'He said nothing.'

'Not, "Oh! Your skin is beautiful"?'

'Nothing.'

'He didn't say any sweet words?'

'Please,' I said, 'I want to go to bed. I want to sleep.' I tried to stand up, but wobbled as I stood, and sank back into my chair.

'Poor thing,' said the woman across the other side of the room, for a second time.

'Perhaps,' suggested Bapak Rerebain gently, 'he said some sweet words, but you did not hear?'

'Perhaps,' I conceded.

'Or he fixed you with a sweet look?'

'Maybe.' I looked down at the floor. Ibu Lin leaned forwards and glowered at me. She jutted out her chin and her eyes became large.

'Beware of his sweet words,' she said, holding up a finger in warning. 'His words sound sweet, but they are filled with poison.'

Bapak Rerebain raised his hand to quieten her. '*Tuan*, do not be angry with us,' he said gently. 'We should have warned you. That old man in the bamboo house is a *suangi*. He is a witch.'

A witch. A soul without anchor. I shook my head. 'No,' I said. 'I'm just sick.'

'You have been attacked by a witch,' Bapak Rerebain said firmly. 'You really should have taken more care. We're ashamed that you should suffer this whilst you are a guest in our house. We do not want you to think that it is we who have hurt you.'

'No, I know,' I said. 'I know it is not your fault.'

Then Ibu Lin broke in. 'Do not worry,' she said. 'We know how to cure you. We will make you better.'

Then Bapak Rerebain went across the room to the corner cupboard, which he opened. He took out a small, insignificant looking piece of wood, and he placed it on the table in front of me. A murmur of approval ran through the room.

'This will cure you,' he said.

A hot root. His *kekuatan mata rumah*.

Bapak Rerebain gave the piece of wood to his wife, Ibu Lin, and she scraped at it with the knife she used to cut up her betel nut, making a little pile of shavings on the tabletop. She called to someone to go and get a glass of water. A woman went off into the kitchen and returned with a half-full glass. Ibu Lin took the glass and put it on the table. Then Bapak Rerebain took the glass and carefully scraped the shavings into the water with the blade of the knife. As he did so, he muttered in

Yamdenan. He stirred the concoction three times clockwise and three times anticlockwise with his knife. As he did so, he glanced at me with uncertainty. Finally he cut the water in the form of a cross.

'I am making a cross,' he said, 'so that Jesus will help us, too.'

As the wood shavings were settling into the bottom of the glass, he laid the knife over the top and covered the knife and glass with his hands. The old man who had been responsible for my diagnosis coughed gently, and rolled his head back on his neck so that he was looking up at the ceiling. Then the old man opened his palms slightly and began to mutter in prayer. The protracted vowel sounds blended into each other almost seamlessly so that his prayer sounded like one long exhalation. One by one, all the other people present joined in. They did not pray in unison, but instead recited their words independently of each other, so that the room filled with a mass of interlocking voices. The sound of their prayers was disorientating. I closed my eyes and the room began to spin. It was as if there was nothing anywhere to take hold of, nothing solid. I was a boat far from land. Gnawed hollow, cut free, adrift on endless seas of nausea as wave after wave of sickness broke over me.

The prayers ended abruptly. I opened my eyes. Bapak Rerebain gave me the glass.

'Take three sips,' he told me.

I picked up the glass and took a sip. The water tasted bitter. I took a second sip and then a third. I closed my eyes. *I'm going to be sick*, I thought.

Bapak Rerebain took the glass and dribbled some water onto my head. He made the sign of the cross on my forehead, presumably to make sure that Jesus was still on board. Then he did the same on my chest. Next he put the glass down and started to press my body at the joints, from the top to the bottom. He worked quickly, pressing his thumbs into my neck, my armpits, my elbows, my groin and my knees. Finally, he took the glass containing the remaining water outside and, with a shout, threw the water into the road. In a few moments, the water had already evaporated.

When he came back inside, he smiled. 'You will be feeling better,' he told me.

I shook my head.

Ibu Lin tutted. 'You already look better,' she said. 'Your face is now pink. You feel better.' It was not a question. It was an order.

'I feel sick,' I said.

A hint of uncertainty entered Ibu Lin's voice. 'Yes,' she said, 'but you feel *a little* better.'

I did not answer. I was battling the nausea that was rising in me as the water and wood shavings worked their way down towards my stomach. I could hear the other guests discussing with relief the success of my cure.

Ibu Lin was saying to anyone who would listen, 'He is better. Look at his pink face. Before he was pale and white, and now he is healthy again.'

Then I was on my feet, running from the room, scattering the chickens that were pecking around in the porch. Leaning against the doorpost, I was violently sick in the road.

When I had finished retching, my body went ice cold. I started to shiver and staggered back into the house. To my surprise, everyone was beaming with undisguised delight.

'See,' said Bapak Rerebain, smiling more broadly than I had seen him smile in days, 'the cure is working.'

The excitement over, the crowd dispersed. Ibu Lin, convinced I was now well on the way to a full recovery, fed me some dry biscuits, but I could not force them down.

'It is good that you are now well,' she kept repeating.

I returned to my bed, and slipped into jumbled dreams. I slept for a long time and woke the following day, long after the sun had risen.

Ӿ

When I woke, I was still sick and giddy. I got up and breakfasted on dry biscuits and a few sips of tea. It was clear that I was still unwell. Ibu Lin and Bapak Rerebain made no comment about the exorcism of the day before, but Bapak Rerebain's face was more deeply furrowed with worry. I went back to bed, and as I lay there I could hear my hosts arguing in the room next door about my illness. Thinking back now, after all these years, I wonder if they were terrified I might not recover at all.

A couple of days later, Bapak Rerebain spoke with me again. By this time, my sickness seemed to be in abeyance a little. I had recovered my appetite enough to take some food, and the fever, although it had not entirely gone, had eased for a while. I was sitting in the front of the house drinking tea with Bapak Rerebain. The tea was managing to stay down in my stomach, and it was warming.

Bapak Rerebain smiled at me. 'Your sickness is not witchcraft,' he said softly. 'We are sorry. We made a mistake.'

'Then what is it?'

'*Masuk angin*,' he said.

'Oh,' I said. '*Masuk angin*.'

There is no more uniquely Indonesian ailment than *masuk angin*. Literally, it means 'wind has entered', and whilst most Indonesian–English dictionaries translate *masuk angin* as 'to catch a cold', this definition is hardly adequate. *Masuk angin* is – potentially at least – a more serious kind of illness. In Tanimbar, the term means precisely what it says: winds in Tanimbar bring in their wake good fortune and ill, health and sickness. There are winds that are constant and steady, good for sailing and healthy for the body. Then there are winds that are fickle and changeable, particularly when the hot season begins to give way to the rainy season, or the day gives way to the night. These winds are dangerous, and bring disease and all kinds of disaster in their train.

'The other day,' Bapak Rerebain said, 'when you were sitting outside, the winds were changing. This is why you are sick. The wind has entered your body, and is now blowing about here and there making you ill. But don't worry. I can cure you.'

In Java and Bali, the usual cure for *masuk angin* is *kerokan*, a process which involves scraping with a coin at the skin of the back, or the back of the neck, so that the excess wind might be released. I had not suffered *kerokan*, although I was told that it was not particularly painful. It did, however, leave behind striking red weals. However, Bapak Rerebain had a different approach to this ailment.

'I will cure you,' he said, somewhat ominously, 'but it might hurt a little.' Then he stood up and put his hands to either side of my head.

'What are you going to do?' I asked.

Bapak Rerebain did not reply. His face became serious and he started to press at the sides of my head. He hunched his shoulders and squeezed as hard as he could. Although he was of slight build, he was remarkably strong.

'Please!' I said. 'Stop.' I tried to struggle free, but was weakened by days of sickness.

Bapak Rerebain, like all good doctors, knew that sometimes it was necessary to endure a little pain in the interests of a cure. 'Hold still,' he said, and increased the pressure.

I knew that there was nothing that I could do. My body went slack. I could feel his hands to either side of my head, pressing harder and harder. It was painful, but it was not the pain that disturbed me so much as the absurd, alarming thought that perhaps my skull would cave in under the pressure.

Bapak Rerebain gave a final grunt and squeeze, then he released me. 'There,' he said. 'Done.'

I looked down at the floor, glowering. I felt violated and angry. My head was sore.

'Drink your tea,' he said kindly.

I took a sip. Then I looked at Bapak Rerebain and saw concern so deeply etched on his face that my anger dissipated. 'Thank you,' I said.

'I am sorry to hurt you,' he said, 'but I am sure you will now get better.'

☥

As it happened, the diagnosis of *masuk angin* also turned out to be wide of the mark, and it took one more cure before I was back on my feet. In the days after the head squeezing, my health fluctuated, getting now better, now worse – but the general direction was towards the worse. Once again I could no longer keep food down, could no longer eat. I just lay on the bed all day, sweating and trembling. The anxious murmurings of my kind, worried hosts were a constant backdrop to my feverish dreams.

Then, one day, Ibu Lin came to speak with me. She sat down gently on the bed, and put her hand on my arm. '*Anak saya*,' she said to me. 'My child.'

I tried to smile at her.

She leaned towards me. 'I know the reason for your sickness,' she said.

'You do?'

She hesitated. '*Sawang*,' she said.

'*Sawang*?' The word was unfamiliar to me.

'Yes, *sawang*. You will not know about *sawang*, because only we people in Tanimbar know about it.'

'What is *sawang*?'

'It is a kind of insect,' Ibu Lin said. Then she explained the cause of my sickness. The *sawang*, she said, was known only to the Tanimbarese. It was not known to Western science. It was an insect, but it came in two forms. The first was an insect in the form of a human being, and the second an insect in the form of an octopus. Whatever form it took,

— 126 —

the *sawang* was usually docile. It resided in the stomach, and it didn't ordinarily cause harm to anyone. But from time to time it would wake and cause trouble.

'This is what has happened to you,' Ibu Lin said. 'Your *sawang* has woken up. It is a *sawang* in the form of an octopus, and it is draining blood from your stomach. If it is not treated, then you could die. But don't worry, I can cure you.'

'You can? How?'

'Massage,' Ibu Lin said, and she yanked up my shirt to expose my belly.

Later I wondered if, in some feverish delirium, I had invented the story about the stomach-octopus. Although *sawang* is recognised as an illness elsewhere in Maluku – where it is associated with bathing in cold rivers, and where the most common symptoms are stomach ache, jaundice and sometimes even, as Ibu Lin had said, death – when I later came to look into it more deeply, I could find no references to its association with octopuses of the stomach. Perhaps, I thought, I had misunderstood Ibu Lin's meaning. But then, years after returning from Indonesia, I read Pat Barker's novel *The Ghost Road*, and there, across a gulf of almost a hundred years and several hundred miles, I came across a strange parallel.

Barker's novel is based in part on the notes of the psychologist and anthropologist W.H.R. Rivers, who was involved in the Torres Strait expedition of 1898. In Barker's book, there is a meeting between Rivers and a medicine man, Njiru:

Meanwhile Rivers and Njiru talked. Namboko Taru's complaint belonged to a group of illnesses called *tagosoro*, which were inflicted by the spirit called Mateana. This particular condition – *nggasin* – was caused by an octopus that had taken up residence in the lower intestine, from where its tentacles might spread until they reached the throat. At this point the disease would prove fatal.

This fictionalised encounter can be traced back to a chapter on 'Massage in Melanesia' in Rivers' 1926 book, *Psychology and Ethnology*. In his book, Rivers claims that massage is used to shrink and eventually kill the stomach-octopus. 'Njiru was a good doctor,' Barker writes, 'however many octopi he located in the colon.'

And so too was Ibu Lin.

Looking at my exposed belly, Ibu Lin smiled a terrible smile. It was a matter of great fortune, she said, that I was staying in her house. She was skilled in the pacification of stomach insects, and had saved a good many lives thereby.

Then she leaned over my prostrate body and, sucking in her breath, she tensed herself like an overweight cat preparing to pounce. She began to pummel my stomach with her podgy fingers, pressing her thumbs hard into the softest parts. Something beneath her thumbs was pulsing and beating.

'See!' she exclaimed, triumphant, her face lighting up. 'I have found it. Can you feel the insect breathing?' Then Ibu Lin made a noise, imitating the pulse. *Bu-DUM. Bu-DUM. Bu-DUM.* 'Can you feel it?'

I could certainly feel it. I nodded, gasping for breath. My hands flailed, ineffectually trying to fend her off. Ibu Lin jabbed her fingers sharply down into my stomach and I yelled out in pain, my knees jerking upwards out of an instinct for self-preservation. Ibu Lin sought out the sensitive point again, and gave it another sharp jab. She hesitated, catching her breath.

'One more,' she said, 'and then you will be well.'

She plunged her fingers sharply downwards one last time, and then released them. I lay gasping on the bed. Sweat had broken out on my forehead. I was shaking with misery and with pain. Ibu Lin looked at me with sympathy and, putting her hand on my forehead in a motherly fashion, gave me a genuinely beautiful smile.

'I will get you a cup of tea,' she said.

X

When I woke the following morning, after the first good sleep I had had in days, I felt better. The *sawang*, or whatever it was, seemed to have been temporarily pacified. I got up and ate breakfast. We were back to the three-egg routine. I ate what I could. Ibu Lin and Bapak Rerebain both smiled to see me eating properly for the first time in days.

'You are lucky,' Bapak Rerebain said as I ate breakfast. 'You are lucky that you got sick in our household, where we know how to treat you.'

And just at that precise moment, as I looked at my two hosts and at the expressions of relief on their face – for all my scepticism when it came to *suangis*, *masuk angin* and *sawangs* – I felt fortunate to be within their care.

12

MANDI ADAT

I spent the next couple of days recovering my strength and my appetite before I felt ready to go and visit Abraham again. By now, I was sure, the sculpture would be nearly finished. I looked forward to seeing it.

When I arrived at Abraham's house, he was putting the finishing touches to the carving, sitting on the floor, working on the sculpture with his fish-skin file. He looked up when I came in, and we shook hands.

'So, you have recovered?' he said.

His tone was not particularly friendly. A kind of chill had come over Abraham, as if something in him had shifted. I had the distinct impression that his question was not motivated by concern, but by convention.

'Luckily, yes,' I replied.

He shrugged. 'There are many strange things in Tanimbar. There are many things you do not understand.' Then he turned the sculpture upright. 'The work is almost finished,' he said. His voice was flat, matter-of-fact.

The *sori luri* was almost perfect. 'It is a beautiful sculpture,' I murmured.

Abraham grunted in reply, but said nothing.

'So we must have a *mandi adat*?' I asked.

Abraham bit his lip, and scratched his neck for a while. 'Perhaps tomorrow,' he suggested cautiously. 'The sculpture will be finished tomorrow, so let us say tomorrow evening. You must go and tell Bapak

Rerebain. He will know what to do. It is difficult for you, because you are a foreigner, but if you listen to Bapak Rerebain, you will not come to any harm.' Abraham picked up the file again.

I waited. There was something not right, something that set me on edge. Abraham wanted me to go. He didn't want to talk.

'I will see you tomorrow,' he said, without looking at me. 'Thank you for coming.'

It was clear that I was being dismissed. I thanked the sculptor and left.

ꭓ

Bapak Rerebain was at the school until the middle of the afternoon. I spent the afternoon reading and making notes. I had been unsettled by Abraham's coldness, and had an uneasy feeling about the *mandi adat*. What if the exchange turned sour? What if things didn't work out?

When Bapak Rerebain returned that afternoon, we talked about the forthcoming ritual. My host did not seem very troubled.

'It will be fine,' he said. 'The important thing is that you do not say anything at all. We will be speaking in Yamdenan, and you will not understand anything. It will be better if you sit quietly and say nothing. If you say anything it might make bad *adat*. Just do as I tell you, and we will be all right. Now, go and buy some palm-wine for the ceremony and bring it back here. After that, everything will be all right. Let me handle everything else.'

There was a tiny store at the end of the street where they sold palm-wine. I walked down the road and bought a bottle.

'Palm-wine?' the man in the shop said. 'For the *mandi adat* with Abraham, or for drinking?' I had not met him before, but clearly news about what was happening had got around the village.

'For the *mandi adat*,' I said.

The shopkeeper laughed and handed over the bottle. I handed over some cash. Then I returned to the house, pleased with my purchase.

Later that evening, over dinner, Bapak Rerebain spoke to me again. 'When we go down to Abraham's house tomorrow, make sure that you do everything exactly as I tell you.' There was a hint of strain in his voice. I reassured him that I would do my best.

After we finished dinner, Bapak Rerebain was preoccupied. I sat and tried to read, but found it hard to concentrate. I was worried about the following day.

Midway through the evening, a messenger came up the hill and spoke in Yamdenan with Bapak Rerebain. Ibu Lin and I were sitting in the front room, chatting. We both watched the conversation unfold – Ibu Lin scowling and grimacing, me trying to look thoughtful and intelligent, even though I didn't understand a single word. As the messenger spoke, Bapak Rerebain's expression changed in a way that made me uncomfortable.

When the messenger left, Bapak Rerebain sat down next to me. He didn't say anything for a long time. He just hunched in his chair. Then he sighed.

'It is like this,' he said. Then he paused. 'Abraham has asked for money.'

'He's asked for money? How much?'

Bapak Rerebain shrugged and his voice dropped to a whisper. 'Two hundred dollars,' he said.

Ibu Lin spat on the ground in disgust. 'Abraham is greedy,' she said. 'He has palm-wine, he has the cork, he has *loran*, and he has some money as a gift. But then he asks for two hundred dollars. Even if it was five dollars, even one dollar, you should not give the money to him. He said that the sculpture would be a gift, and now he asks for money, so it is no gift at all.'

Bapak Rerebain looked embarrassed. 'I am sorry. Abraham said it would be a gift, and now he asks for money. He says he is making a *walut*, but he sells it like a sack of rice. This is bad *adat*.'

'So, what should I do?' I asked.

Bapak Rerebain sighed. 'The choice is yours. But it is better if we do not go ahead,' he said. 'It would be dangerous for you, and it would be dangerous for us. If you don't want to proceed, I will tell Abraham that you do not accept, that you will only accept the sculpture as a gift.'

Ibu Lin and Bapak Rerebain looked at me in silence, waiting for me to respond. I looked back at them, unsure what I should or could say. I had not expected things to go awry with Abraham. I wanted to go ahead with the *mandi adat*. Not just because of the sculpture, but also because I was interested, because I wanted to see what would happen. But then I looked at my hosts, and I saw the unease on their faces, and I knew that I could not involve them in a venture to which they were so firmly opposed.

'Okay,' I said. 'Let's tell Abraham that we can't continue.'

So Bapak Rerebain sent word to Abraham that I understood the sculpture to have been made as a gift, and would only accept it in that spirit. He said that, were the sculpture to be offered again as a gift, I would make sure that my counter-gift was generous. But, he concluded, I would only accept the *walut* as a gift, for it had been a gift in turn, a gift from the ancestors.

Over the next couple of days, negotiations continued from a distance, messengers going to and fro between Ibu Lin and Bapak Rerebain's house and Abraham's house. Bapak Rerebain tried to get the sculptor to withdraw his demand, tried to reassure him that if the gift exchange went ahead I would be sufficiently generous to make it worth his while. But this transaction had become a matter of *adat* ritual law and local politics, and I felt out of my depth. Bapak Rerebain told me every so often that I shouldn't worry, that everything would be all right. But he did not look convinced.

I had no option other than to let things take their course. Whilst negotiations were still underway, Bapak Rerebain forbade me from going to speak to Abraham.

'You must not speak with him until this is resolved,' he said. 'Otherwise he will think that you are agreeing to his demands. You must leave everything to us.'

Bapak Rerebain didn't speak with him directly either. In fact, everything was conducted through intermediaries. Messengers came and went, and gradually the sum for which Abraham was asking plummeted. But, each time, Bapak Rerebain explained that I could only accept the sculpture as a gift, and that I would not negotiate on any other terms.

After two days, the messenger came with his final offer: three thousand rupiah, upfront. A dollar and a half. I felt ashamed by this pitifully small amount. It was far less than the counter-gift I had planned to give after the *mandi adat*.

'No,' Bapak Rerebain said. 'We will not accept a price of three thousand rupiah. The sculpture was a gift, and a gift had no price.'

The messenger slunk away to pass on the news.

X

It was then that I had an idea. I was becoming sick of the protracted wranglings. I wanted to bring things to a conclusion.

'What if,' I said to Bapak Rerebain, 'I paid the three thousand rupiah upfront, as a guarantee of good will? And what if we then went through the *mandi adat*, after which I could present Abraham with a much more substantial gift?'

Abraham would be more than satisfied. Ibu Lin and Bapak Rerebain would save face. I would be able to take the gift home. It was a solution that would suit everyone.

But I hadn't thought about the ancestors. Bapak Rerebain sighed and rubbed his eyes. 'If you wish,' he said, 'we can do it like this. But *adat* is not buying and selling. Abraham made the sculpture as a gift. How can it be a gift if he asks for money? It is not that the money is too much. It is that this is bad *adat*.'

It was a matter of the *taste* of the thing. There is a beautiful passage in McKinnon's ethnography in which she asks a Tanimbarese friend, Falaksoru Ditilebit, why one should bother with exchange at all. Bapak Ditilebit replies that the reason one bothers is because exchange is *manminak* – it is 'tasty'. The point of exchange, Bapak Ditilebit says, is not to make profit, but instead to 'look for relation'.

McKinnon goes on to say that one condition for an exchange being *manminak*, one condition for its 'tastiness', is that those who are party to an exchange 'know the system and understand how to play it'. When I now look back on this botched exchange with Abraham Amelwatin, it seems to me that there was something lacking in tastiness, something perhaps even *tasteless*, in the situation in which we all found ourselves – myself, Abraham and my hosts, the Rerebains. I had been drawn into the heart of a system that I did not know how to play. My involvement was causing havoc. It was a disaster.

All this is why, on Bapak Rerebain's advice, late in the afternoon of what was to be my final day in Alusi Krawain, I refused Abraham's final offer.

'No,' Bapak Rerebain said to the messenger. 'He will only accept the *walut* as a gift. We cannot discuss this any more. The sculpture was made as a gift and should remain a gift. If Abraham wants to change his mind, he must tell us, and then we can conduct proper *adat*. If we do so, I can guarantee that he will receive a generous gift in return.'

The messenger disappeared and did not return. By the evening, it was clear that things were not going to go ahead. Abraham had lost faith in the *mandi adat*. He had lost faith in me.

We were all subdued that evening. Ibu Lin and her husband were weary. It was so very different from that first night in Alusi Krawain, when Ibu Lin and I had strutted and danced to the yelping of Tom Waits.

'We have failed you,' Bapak Rerebain said quietly. 'And so you must go. I am very sorry you will be leaving Alusi Krawain empty handed.'

I reminded them of their hospitality and their kindness. I said that even if I was to leave Alusi Krawain empty handed, I would not be leaving empty hearted. In Indonesian you can say things like that without sounding trite. But on this occasion, it fell flat.

'If Abraham does not respond, there is no point in you staying here any longer,' said Bapak Rerebain. 'Your journey to Alusi Krawain has been wasted, and it would be better were you to return to Saumlaki.'

Ibu Lin nodded. 'You must go!' she told me. 'Why stay here wasting your time? You have work to do. You must come and visit us again if you have time, but for now you must go. There is a bus tomorrow to Saumlaki, and we will make sure you have a place on it.'

The following morning, the messenger reappeared to confirm that Abraham had refused the offer. The bus back to Saumlaki was leaving just after noon. Ibu Lin and Bapak Rerebain, perhaps to hasten my departure, announced they were travelling south to visit their daughter, and that I should accompany them. Their air of disappointment was palpable. Suddenly I felt as if I didn't belong there in Alusi Krawain. Ibu Lin Rerebain, who had talked of me as a son, was now awkward with me. It was as if the failure of the *adat* had highlighted the sad fact that I had no place there, as if it had demonstrated the falsity of Ibu

Lin's hope that somehow I could truly be a member of the Rerebain household. And how could there be *adat*, how could there be exchange, when I would inevitably leave, as all outsiders and strangers eventually left, trailing behind me tatters of broken relationships, rents in a torn and threadbare fabric?

It was not *manminak*. It was not tasty. It was bad *adat*.

On that final morning, when I got up and sat eating breakfast with Ibu Lin and Bapak Rerebain – Roki lurking under the table keeping a surreptitious eye out for falling eggs – I realised I had become a stranger again. I was a problem, somebody who needed to be escorted away from the village before I caused further damage. What business did I have, after all, getting myself tangled up in *adat* transactions? No amount of heirloom gold, no number of libations of palm-wine, no prayers and offerings could disguise the fact that I did not belong. And what other option did Abraham have? It was as if he had been the first to see through the charade of my involvement in the *mandi adat*. You don't do *adat* with outsiders. Abraham could not really be blamed. What option did he have, other than to re-imagine our transaction not as *adat*, but as a simple trade?

Towards noon, I asked Ibu Lin and Bapak Rerebain if I could go and speak to Abraham, to thank him for his time, to say goodbye, but with an angry forcefulness that I had not seen in him before, Bapak said no.

'He wishes to conduct bad *adat*, so you must not speak with him unless he changes his mind. There is still time. If he decides to offer the sculpture again as a gift, then we can talk to him. Otherwise, we must go.'

We ate lunch more or less in silence. Ibu Lin tried to be cheerful, but I could sense she wanted rid of me. I went to pack my bags.

As we waited for the bus by the side of the road, I wondered how the sculpture had turned out. I regretted that I would never see it. But, more than this, I regretted the fact that I could not say goodbye to Abraham, this sculptor of extraordinary talents.

A group of well-wishers from the village came to wish me a good trip. Soon the bus arrived, churning its way through the dust on the road that led from the villages to the north.

Ibu Lin and Bapak Rerebain got on board. I was about to follow when a man stepped out of the crowd to shake my hand. I recognised him as one of those I had sat with in the darkness of Abraham's house while the sculptor carved the block of wood held between his feet.

'Goodbye,' he said, clasping my hand. 'I am sorry you're leaving without the sculpture.'

I smiled at him. 'It doesn't matter,' I said, trying to sound magnanimous. 'Please, send my good wishes to Abraham.'

'Abraham is a fool,' he said. 'What use is a sculpture? It is just a block of wood. And you can't eat wood.' He paused. 'Abraham will be the one who suffers, you know. That *walut* was made as a gift, but he tried to sell it. He made bad *adat*. The ancestors will punish him.'

'I should go,' I said. 'The bus is leaving.'

He let go of my hand. 'Abraham,' he said, 'will turn into a block of wood, like his useless sculpture. His body will become stiff, and he will die.' Then he smiled and wished me a good trip.

I climbed the steps into the bus and found a seat behind Ibu Lin and Bapak Rerebain. We started to rattle our way down the road back to Saumlaki. I looked out of the window as we passed the village square, the outlying houses. Soon we were on the road that cut through the forest.

I closed my eyes, and thought of Abraham sitting in the darkness of his house, the *walut* by his side, and I thought of him slowly turning into a block of wood as the lizards chattered noisily in the rafters, speaking the obscure and almost-forgotten language of the ancestors: *to-kek, to-kek, to-kek.*

PART IV

JAMAN MODEREN

THE MODERN AGE

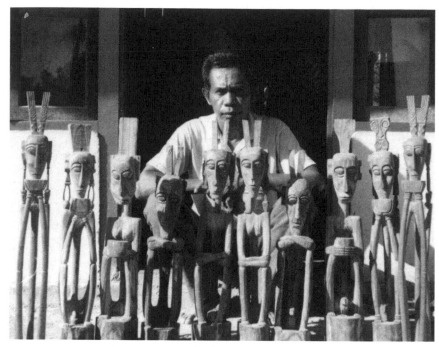

Damianus Masele, from Tumbur, Yamdena

13

THE OLD SONGS

Back in Saumlaki, I spent one more night in the Harapan Indah, then I moved out and rented a room from Ibu Neli in Olilit Baru, just on the outskirts of town. Ibu Neli lived with her son Lucky in a small, comfortable house. Behind the house was a yard with a small *mandi* or washroom. It was cheaper than the hotel, and more comfortable. Ibu Neli had set up a small room for me – a section of the living room cordoned off by a curtain, with a bed, a window and a small chest for keeping my belongings, as well as a desk by the window at which I could work. It was a homely place, and Ibu Neli turned out to be a considerate and solicitous host.

Despite the fact that Olilit Baru had a reputation for witchcraft, I found the village a good place to be. It was quieter than the Harapan Indah, but the walk into town was easy. Tanimbarese friends were far more at ease visiting me there; most local people felt ill at ease in the hotel. And there was the pleasure of having a space where I too felt at home.

Sometimes I wandered down to the Harapan Indah hotel to see what was happening, who had arrived recently, who had left and what the latest gossip was. I enjoyed visiting the Harapan Indah. It was a hub of rumour, a place where government officials and foreign businessmen rubbed shoulders with mining engineers, speculators and ornithologists here in search of the Tanimbar megapode, a brownish pheasant-like bird known for its shy nature. It was useful to be aware of what was going on in the Tanimbar Islands, to pick up on news. But it was also good to have a home away from the hotel, a place where I could settle down and do some serious work.

I had an interim report to write for the Indonesian Institute of Sciences, so I borrowed Pastor Böhm's typewriter, a heavy black machine, with solid, clunky keys. I bought a ream of cheap paper from a shop in the market, and I spent a contented few weeks writing up notes to the satisfying *clack-clack-clack* of the typewriter. When I became weary of writing notes, I entertained myself by writing stories. After weeks of speaking only Indonesian, it was a relief to use my native language, and I took immense pleasure in simply putting words on the page.

Ϫ

One day, as I was sitting at my desk working, Benny Fenyapwain came to visit. He had with him an old cassette recorder.

'This will interest you,' he said.

I went and made tea for us both. When I returned, Benny had set up the cassette recorder on the table.

'What have you got?' I asked him.

'A singer from Sifnana,' he said. 'He was one of Tanimbar's finest singers. Listen – '

Benny pressed play. There was a background hiss, and then the sound of a drum: three beats, the third stressed, followed by a pause, the fourth beat left silent.

Bom... Bom... BOM... Pause... Bom... Bom... BOM... Pause...

The tape was of low quality, but in the background I could hear a murmur of voices. I closed my eyes. I could imagine the smoke-filled room, the drinking of palm-wine, the murmur of conversation.

The drum continued until the voices subsided; then, once the conversation died away, I heard the voice of an old man – feeble and wavering

– as he broke into song. Although the voice was cracked by years of drinking palm-wine and smoking clove cigarettes, it carried a measured, sustained passion.

Benny translated from Yamdenan to Indonesian. I scribbled notes in English. The song opened:

I alone know the old songs;
I alone sing the old songs.
They say I am mad,
they no longer listen,
but who will sing these songs when I am dead?
What will happen to these songs when I am gone?

The singer improvised freely, punctuating his singing with the occasional spoken aside, his song meandering without any certain pattern or design. Benny stopped the tape occasionally for me to jot down further notes. The old man sang about the past, about the future and about the virtues of palm-wine. Palm-wine made a man's body strong, he sang. It gave him courage and power, made his muscles taut. The palm-wine from Sifnana was better than the palm-wine from Ilngei. It was more delicious than the palm-wine from Sangliat. It was stronger than the palm-wine from Olilit. It was the finest palm-wine in Tanimbar. It was the finest palm-wine in the world.

The recording came to an end. Benny switched the machine off. 'This singer,' he said, 'was very well known.'

'Can we go and see him?' I asked. Sifnana was not far away.

'He is dead,' Benny said. 'He died ten years ago.'

Ӿ

A few days later, Benny and I went to Sifnana, although not in search of palm-wine or singers. Instead we were there to visit a sculpture that I was interested in. The sculpture was just to the side of the road out of Saumlaki, overlooking the bay, in the exact place where the Dutch pastors Cappers and Klerks first landed on the Tanimbar Islands. I had spotted it a few times from the bus on my journeys towards the north, and I wanted to take a closer look.

Benny gave me a lift on his motorbike. The sculpture was a substantial monument fashioned out of concrete in the form of a triptych. Set into the wings to either side were little windows through which it was possible to look out to sea. In the centre was a relief depicting the Dutch pastors skimming over the surface of a choppy sea teeming with wildlife. The sculptor, Benny said, was famous for his works in concrete.

I looked at the relief. Beneath the priests' boat, there was a black smudge – a turtle rising to the surface, as if in recognition of the Dutchmen's holiness, or intent on receiving their blessing. The pastors were dressed for the job, whiskers quivering in anticipation, one holding a

cross up against the blue sky, the other with his back ramrod straight, a copy of the Bible in his open hand.

There are strange parallels between the story of Atuf and his siblings and the story of Cappers and Klerks. Atuf came from the west; so did Cappers and Klerks. Atuf brought a magical spear, and by wielding this spear he re-fashioned time and history; the priests brought a magical cross, and through the power of this cross they made the world anew. The *jaman purba* gave way to the *jaman pertengahan* thanks to the spear. The *jaman pertengahan* gave way to the *jaman moderen* thanks to the cross. The parallels are exact, up to a point – because, if it is true that history repeats itself, it is also true that with each repetition it improvises and reinvents; it takes ancient themes and dreams them afresh.

The next village I was intending to visit was Tumbur, the most famous woodcarving village in Tanimbar. I had seen carvings from Tumbur – they were elegant and slender, carved out of *kayu hitam*, or black ebony – not only in shops and houses around Saumlaki, but also in Ambon and in the Netherlands. The sculptors of Tumbur were not lone, maverick artists like Abraham and Matias; instead, sculpture in Tumbur was an impressively well-organised cottage industry.

However, before travelling to Tumbur, I had other business to attend to. The bureaucratic demands of the Indonesian state were no less binding and complex than the *adat* demands of the ancestors. The fistful of permits that permitted me to carry out research in Tanimbar were in need of renewal, and I had to return to submit my interim report to the Indonesian Institute of Sciences. Not only this, but – as I obsessively related in letters sent home – I was fast running out of cash, and I was several hundred kilometres away from the nearest bank where I could exchange money.

I booked a flight back to Ambon. It was early December. I intended to spend Christmas and New Year in Ambon before flying back to Tanimbar. I was not much looking forward to spending long hours in government offices, filling in paperwork, but by way of compensation I had an invitation to celebrate New Year with my friend Paay Suripatty and his wife, Tin.

I had met Paay a few weeks before in the Harapan Indah, and we had shared a few beers. Paay was employed by an organisation that worked on small development projects throughout Maluku, and he was entertaining company: generous hearted, spirited in conversation, passionate about telling jokes. He said that when I was next in Ambon I should come and visit him and Tin. I told him that I would be there over New Year, and so he invited me up to celebrate the festival with them. They had built their own house in the forest outside of Ambon, and Paay said that it was a paradise of sorts. They washed in the stream that ran past their door, and spent their days taking it easy, eating pineapples, rambutan and gandaria, the exquisite small mangoes that you can eat skin and all.

'Come and celebrate New Year,' Paay said. 'We'll drink beer and eat fruit and relax.'

It was a tempting offer. I flew back to Ambon in late December, and took a taxi into town.

✗

It was strange to be back in the city. Everything seemed vast and sprawling. I booked into a hotel, joking with the receptionist that, after so long in Tanimbar, Ambon felt like New York.

The next couple of weeks passed in a blur of drab offices and moulding documents. On Christmas Day, I ate dinner at a solitary street stall, and found somewhere to make a phone call home. Then I headed back to the hotel, where I got drunk with a businessman from the Aru Islands called Frankie.

Frankie was a dark, serious-looking man in his early forties, his hair already turning grey. He approached me with a greeting that approximated to 'Merry Christmas', and invited me to have a drink. When he found out I could speak Indonesian, he was delighted. We sat in the hotel lobby and drank our way through several beers. Frankie said that he was glad to be spending Christmas drinking with an Englishman because – as he told me after two beers – several years ago he had spent some time in England.

'Oh,' I said. 'Where have you been?'

'Berwick,' he told me, pronouncing 'Berwick' with a sharply rolled 'r'. 'Berwick-upon-Tweed.'

'Where else? London? Edinburgh? Newcastle?'

'Nowhere,' he said. 'Nowhere else. Only Berwick-upon-Tweed.'

The story went something like this: Frankie had arrived in Berwick with a suitcase full of pearls. The Aru Islands were famous for their pearls, which were both large and of high quality. Frankie had amassed a large collection, and through an intermediary he had arranged a voyage on a container ship to England. He had no passport and no visa. When officials came on board the ship, he hid.

The voyage was a long one, but eventually the boat put into dock in the tiny port of Berwick-upon-Tweed. ('Berwick is a beautiful town,' he told me.) Frankie arranged to meet the English buyers in the town. They took the pearls and ran, giving him nothing in return. Frankie – without passport, money or any command of English – fled back to the boat. He managed to negotiate an exchange of his labour for a passage home.

Nevertheless, despite his suffering at the hands of the duplicitous

English criminals, he maintained a deep affection for England and for the English.

'The English people are good,' he said, 'they are kind. But there are bad people everywhere.'

It all sounded implausible, and yet Frankie talked of Berwick-upon-Tweed with a familiarity that made it impossible to entirely disbelieve him. Frankie still dealt in pearls – at one point in the evening, he removed a handkerchief from his pocket and showed me a clutch of gleaming white spheres – but he was now more interested in other lines of business. He took from his briefcase a brochure written in Japanese and English. According to the brochure, there were substantial gains to be made on investing in a new theme park that was soon to open outside Tokyo. I looked through the brochure. Everything seemed glossily hyper-real.

'How about we invest together?' Frankie said. 'We can go into business together. I am meeting with the Japanese businessmen in a few days' time. You must join us.'

After several beers, and some spirits of dubious provenance, Frankie invited me to his home in the Aru Islands. By this time he was firmly convinced that we should be collaborators in all future business transactions. With his business skills and connections, and with my English, he was sure that we would become rich. I told him I would think about it. Then we had a final toast in honour of Christmas, after which, feeling drunk and dislocated, I listed off along the corridor and up the stairs to collapse on my bed.

I never saw Frankie again. But on the day after Christmas, Paay and Tin got in touch, and invited me to come and stay up in the forest. I packed my bags and caught a minibus out of town. My friends were waiting by the side of the road, and they flagged down the minibus. I jumped off and followed them down the path that led into the forest for a kilometre or so, until we reached their house.

Everything they had said was true. The house *was* a paradise of sorts. It was made of whitewashed boards that gleamed in the sunlight, and was surrounded by fruit trees. The only downside, as far as I was concerned, was that large black spiders were fond of taking up residence between the boards, and emerging at night to glare at me menacingly.

I spent the few days leading up to New Year reading James George Frazer's *The Golden Bough*. I had picked up an abridged paperback of the book in a small café in Ambon, where it had been abandoned by

STEALING WITH THE EYES

another anthropologically inclined traveller. Up there in the forest, the days slid past blissfully. We sat around chatting and joking, read books, went for walks through the forest to visit friends. Occasionally I had to head into town to sort out bits and pieces of paperwork, but most of the time I just sat on the bench that Paay and Tin had built underneath the gandaria tree, where I read and munched on fruit.

But the more time I spent in the forest outside Ambon, the more my qualms about returning to Tanimbar increased. I thought of Matias and Abraham, both of them in their different ways immobilised – Matias by misfortune and poverty and his broken legs, and Abraham slowly turning to a block of wood on account of the ancestors' wrath. I thought about witchcraft and cures, and about lightness and weight, about gifts and transactions. And then, as I was reading *The Golden Bough*, I came across a passage that brought me up short. It was in the section titled 'The Occasional Expulsion of Evils in a Material Vehicle':

In Timor-laut [Tanimbar], to mislead the demons who are causing sickness, a small proa, containing the image of a man and provisioned for a long voyage, is allowed to drift away with wind and tide. As it is being launched, the people cry, "O sickness, go from here; turn back; what do you here in this poor land?" Three days after this ceremony a pig is killed, and part of the flesh is offered to Dudilaa, who lives in the sun. One of the oldest men says, "Old sir, I beseech you make well the grand-children, children, women, and men, that we may be able to eat pork and rice and to drink palm-wine. I will keep my promise. Eat your share, and make all the people in the village well."

I read this and put the book down.

What sicknesses and discontents, I wondered, had I brought to Tanimbar? And now that I had left, drifting away with wind and tide, what greater discontents would I bring by returning? *What do you here in this poor land?*

These were questions to which I could find no good answers.

X

For New Year, I baked a courgette cake in a tin oven that we perched on top of a Primus stove. The cake was enormous, because Paay and Tin insisted that they had a lot of relatives and friends coming to visit, and so I should not make it too small. The first attempt at making cake batter was a disaster, as when I added the ninth and final egg it turned out to be rotten. The second batter worked better, and we took care to crack the eggs separately first, just to check.

My hosts were sceptical, but when the cake came out of the oven, it was delicious. That evening, the guests arrived. We talked. We played chess. We drank. We ate slabs of cake. And we toasted each other with beer underneath the gandaria tree, as all around us thrummed the racket of the forest by night.

When midnight came, the new year, 1995, was signalled by the flowering of distant fireworks. Down in the bay, we could hear the sound of ships blowing their horns.

As I watched the fireworks blooming in the sky, and listened to the throb of insect life all around us, I thought that perhaps this was paradise. But I knew that I couldn't stay there forever. I had work to do back in Tanimbar. I woke up the following morning hung over, and started to plan my trip back to Saumlaki.

Over the first days of January, I put the remainder of my paperwork in order. I flew back to Saumlaki on the morning of the ninth of January. My generous hosts said goodbye to me, and I took a taxi to the airport. Soon I was chewing on a stale airline bread roll, as the squat little plane to Tanimbar chugged over the Arafura Sea. And by that afternoon I was back in Olilit Baru, with my typewriter, my small desk and my window.

☓

Not long after arriving back in Saumlaki, I paid a visit to the Harapan Indah hotel, to see if I could catch up on the latest gossip. As I was sitting in the reception area, drinking coffee and chatting to Dina, a Westerner appeared through the door of the hotel. I heard him before I saw him. Barefoot and dressed in vest top and shorts, he rattled as he walked, on account of the amulets, totems, strings of beads and other forms of ethnic regalia he had picked up on his global travels and draped around his neck. When he came into the hotel, he nodded at me and said hello. From his accent, I guessed that he was French.

His pale, thin wife followed after him. She was a nervous-looking woman in tie-dyed skirt, blouse and headband. She had the air of a woman who had spent too many years shuttling from ashram to ashram seeking peace and love, and who was beginning to suspect that this was not the way that she might find these things.

The Frenchman sat down and introduced himself. His wife sat next to him, giving me a wan and distant smile, then turned her head away to look into the middle distance. The Frenchman said they had arrived several days before on a passenger boat that had come via Nusa Tenggara. They had spent the last few days visiting the major tourist sites. They had been to see the stone boat at Sangliat Dol, and had visited Tumbur and a number of other villages – and, he said, they were underwhelmed.

'Have you just arrived?' he asked.

'I've just got back,' I said. 'I'm here as an anthropologist. I was in Ambon over Christmas sorting out paperwork.'

The Frenchman looked unimpressed. He leaned towards me. 'You are an anthropologist,' he said. 'But let me tell you what *I* think about Tanimbar.' An anxious smile fluttered across his wife's face.

'Okay,' I said.

'Tanimbar,' he said, 'is shit.' He said it with a long 'ee' sound. 'Tanimbar is *sheet*.'

'Oh,' I said.

'Sheet,' he repeated, in case I had not heard.

We sat in silence for a few moments. 'Let me tell you why Tanimbar is sheet,' the Frenchman continued.

'Go on,' I said.

He indicated towards the Tumburese sculptures that lined the walls of the hotel. 'These people,' he said, 'they make sheet sculptures. They are tourist sheet.'

I had to suppress a sudden and unexpected surge of anger. 'Some of them are very finely carved,' I said.

He looked at me as if I was an idiot and slurped his coffee. 'How long have you been here?'

'Several months,' I said.

'And you like it?'

'It is interesting,' I said. I was glad to be back in Tanimbar, although I still wasn't sure whether I liked it.

The Frenchmen shook his head. The totems around his neck clattered. 'Tanimbar is not interesting. It is sheet. Nobody wears traditional clothes, nobody lives in traditional houses – '

'The Dutch tore down their houses years ago,' I said. 'That's not the fault of the Tanimbarese.'

The Frenchman's wife reached out a tentative hand and touched his arm, but he brushed her to one side. He was becoming red in the face.

'I came here to find culture,' he said, 'but the culture in Tanimbar is dead. The people just waste their time making tourist sheet. These people are not *primitif* any more.'

'*Primitif?*' I said.

He nodded. '*Primitif.*'

'Oh,' I said.

'Tomorrow we are going to Irian Jaya,' he said. 'They still have culture in Irian Jaya.' The Frenchman downed his coffee and shook my hand. 'Good luck,' he said. 'You are wasting your time.' Then he stood and, without looking at his wife, headed out into the street. His wife followed behind, giving me an apologetic smile as she left.

When they had gone, I sat for a while, looking up at the sculptures from the village of Tumbur. With their slender limbs carved from *kayu hitam*, they had been carved with remarkable skill and dexterity. It was high time, I thought, that I paid the village a visit.

14

SELLING HISTORY

One afternoon, as I was making preparations to visit Tumbur, I decided to visit Pastor Böhm. It was late afternoon when I knocked on the door. The priest invited me in. He cracked open a couple of beers and asked me how the work was going. I told him I was visiting Tumbur.

'Ah,' he said. 'Tumbur. I think you will find it interesting. Tumbur is very different from the other places you have been. In Tumbur, they are very organised.' He thought for a while. 'The sculptures are good,' he said, 'but – how should I say this – they are unusual.'

He got up from his chair and went over to the cupboard in the corner, which he opened to take out a number of elegant, fine-limbed figures carved out of black *kayu hitam*. He placed them in a row on the table in front of me. Some figures were squatting with knees drawn up, elbows resting upon their knees. Others were standing, holding machetes or spears. Pastor Böhm handed me one of the sculptures.

I had first seen the sculptures from the village of Tumbur in the Netherlands. From the first it had struck me that there was something strange about them. Aesthetically, at least, they bore no obvious resemblance to the traditions of Tanimbarese art from the earlier part of the twentieth century. I had seen nothing like them in museum collections in Leiden or Utrecht, or in the British Museum. Although the motifs – of boats, of warriors, of women carrying baskets to the gardens in the forest – referenced the traditional past of the Tanimbar Islands, when put alongside Tanimbarese historical works they nevertheless seemed strangely alien.

Up in Alusi Krawain, Abraham Amelwatin had bluntly told me that the work of the Tumburese sculptors was rubbish.

'They know nothing about sculpture over there in Tumbur,' he said. 'They just make things for tourists. They call their sculptures *walut*, but they are not *walut* at all. Only my sculptures are made through the power of the *tetek nenek moyang*.' But Abraham's verdict was as unfair as that of the Frenchman I had met in Saumlaki, for it was hard not to be impressed by the sheer skill and artistry of many Tumburese sculptures, carved from hard wood with nothing more than penknives. For their sheer refinement, the sculptures made in Tumbur were as impressive as anything else I had seen in Tanimbar.

'There are ways you can tell the quality of these works,' Pastor Böhm said. 'You must look at the thinness of the limbs. The thinner the better. But be careful of breaks, because bad sculptors try hard to disguise them with glue and shoe polish. In good sculptures, the hands and feet are also very detailed. Look at the difference between these two.' He pointed to two sculptures. Now that I looked at them, I could see that one was more precisely and carefully crafted than the other.

As I looked at the sculptures, Pastor Böhm told me about the industry in Tumbur. It had started twenty years before, at the instigation of a lay worker of the Catholic church. Two decades on, there were more than one hundred sculptors working in the village, divided into four different *kelompoks* or work groups. This thriving cottage industry brought money and prestige. The village was marked as a tourism development village by the regional government. Things were looking good for Tumbur. They were even building a new church.

'Sculpture has helped people in Tumbur a great deal,' the priest said.

'Why don't other villages follow suit?' I asked him.

Pastor Böhm smiled. 'In other villages they have tried,' he said. 'But every time they try, they give up.'

'Too difficult?'

'No. It is not about difficulty. It is because people are afraid to copy, you know.' He looked at me sideways. 'The people of Tumbur have a reputation, you see – for witchcraft. People elsewhere pick up a chisel, begin to work, get a little sick and then panic. They think this is witchcraft, so they stop working. This happened in Wowonda. A number of sculptors decided to copy what they were doing in Tumbur, but when one of them got sick, they got scared and gave up. They said it was too dangerous.'

'A useful reputation,' I said.

Pastor Böhm smiled and took a swig of beer. 'It is,' he said. 'It is a very useful reputation indeed.' Then the priest sighed. 'When are you going to Tumbur?'

'As soon as possible,' I told him.

'Well, in that case, you must stay in the *pastoran*. It is owned by the Catholic church. If you stay there, you will have peace and quiet. You will be able to work. You can eat with someone in the village, but it will be more peaceful for you to stay in the *pastoran*. I will give you the key.'

I thanked Pastor Böhm for his offer. He went to rummage in a drawer for the key.

'How are you getting to Tumbur?' he asked me.

'Benny has offered to give me a lift.'

'Then you will not have any problem in finding the *pastoran*. It is just opposite the site of the new church. They are still building it. They are planning to fill it with sculptures. I want to encourage them to make traditional carvings, to combine local traditions and Christian iconography. But they are reluctant. I'm afraid they will just make sculptures like the ones in the West. It is a lost opportunity, don't you think?'

I nodded. Then the priest cleared away the sculptures.

'Good,' he said. 'I wish you luck. You will have no problems in Tumbur. They are used to foreigners. Enjoy it!'

Ϫ

The following afternoon, Benny turned up with his motorbike. I climbed on the back and we headed up to Tumbur, taking the highway north and then turning east towards the village. Benny dropped me off at the *pastoran*, a low building with a grass roof and a slightly derelict air, surrounded by a scrubby fenced garden.

Opposite my new home, a group of men was breaking stones with hammers in the hot sun and drinking palm-wine.

'They are building the new church,' Benny grinned. 'When it is complete, it will be very beautiful.'

We went up to the door and I put the key in the lock. To my surprise, it was unlocked. From inside came the sound of rustling. I turned the handle and pushed the door open. There was a gloomy, bare room, the walls painted with multi-coloured scenes of palm trees and beaches.

Then a nun emerged from the room next door, with a questioning look on her face. She was probably in her fifties, and had one tooth missing at the front.

'Can I help you?' she asked.

I held up the key. 'Pastor Böhm gave me the key,' I said. 'I didn't think anybody was here. I'll go and find somewhere else.'

'What are you doing in Tumbur?'

'I'm here to do research. I'm an anthropologist.'

'Then you should have this place to yourself,' she said. 'Wait, I'll get my things.'

I tried to protest, but the nun insisted. She was happy to find another place to stay, she said. She had friends in Wowonda, just down the coast. She would leave me in peace. She gathered up her bags, and left the *pastoran*. Benny and I watched her walk away.

'I feel a bit guilty,' I said to Benny.

He laughed. 'Don't worry,' he said. 'She didn't look too worried.' He looked around at the painted palm trees. They were both lurid and strangely murky. 'Welcome to Tumbur,' he said.

I had a look around the *pastoran*. It was basic. The front room had a swept concrete floor, a large comfortable desk and an upright wooden chair. It looked like a good enough place to write, even though there was not much natural light. Out the back were the remains of what had once been a kitchen, but it was so full of rubble, dust and stones that it was inaccessible. There was a tiny dank bathroom with a tap that dripped constantly, and a background mosquito hum. Finally, there was a small bedroom containing a wooden bed draped with a mosquito net so torn and tattered that it had only a symbolic value. Crouching on the mosquito net was a large, determined-looking black spider.

'Welcome to your new home,' said Benny. 'I'll come back in a few days to see how you are doing.'

I thanked Benny, shook his hand and stood in the doorway of the *pastoran* watching him leave. After he had gone, leaving me there in the grass-thatched cottage amongst the painted palm trees, I felt somehow desolate. I started to unpack.

It soon became apparent that I was very much a minority species in the little house. The spider on the mosquito netting was one of many. The spiders were everywhere – rustling through the woven thatch of the roof, lurking in corners, prowling amongst the rubble in the kitchen. Deciding that there was not enough space in the house for all of us, I spotted a broom in the corner of the bedroom. *I'll chase the spiders away with the broom*, I said to myself. *Then I'll be able to sleep more easily*. But when I got closer to the broom, hunched on its handle I saw yet another spider. We eyed each other warily, then I gave up on my plan. The spiders were too clever for me. They knew my game. I had no choice but to settle for an uneasy truce.

I stacked my books on the desk, took out some mosquito coils for later and tried to make myself comfortable. I was reassured by the sound of a gecko up in the roof somewhere calling out *tok-ek, tok-ek, tok-ek*. *Perhaps it's hungry*, I thought. *Perhaps it eats spiders*.

As I was settling in, there was a knock at the door. A serious-looking man in his forties was standing outside, holding a cap in his hand. He was about my height, and had jet-black hair.

'Welcome to Tumbur,' he said, without smiling.

I invited the visitor in.

He sat down and told me that his name was Damianus. 'I have heard why you are here,' he said. I wondered how he knew. Word travelled fast in Tanimbar. 'I am the best sculptor in the village, so you need to talk to me. I will be able to help you. Other people will say that they are better. They are telling lies.'

He said this without pride, as if it were a fact of nature. Later it turned out that this was neither hyperbole nor false modesty: when I saw his work that evening, I discovered that Damianus was a fine and accomplished artist.

Damianus was head of one of the four *kelompoks* in the village. 'I was one of the first to carve,' he said. 'There were four of us, and we learned together. I will tell you all about this. Come to my house this evening. Whilst you are here in Tumbur, my family will feed you.'

Damianus had an uncompromising air. I suspected that he was not the kind of man with whom one would want to disagree too strongly.

'Thank you,' I said. 'I'd appreciate that.'

'I'll call on you later to bring you to my home,' he said. Then he got up to leave.

Not more than ten minutes after Damianus had left, another man came to the door. He introduced himself, and he too said that he was the finest sculptor in the village.

'Come to my house this evening,' he said. 'We will eat together and we will talk.' I explained that I had already accepted an offer from Damianus. My visitor's face fell, and he left sharply. For the remainder of my stay in Tumbur, he did not speak with me again. When I saw him around the village, he turned his back and refused to speak to me. When it came to local politics in Tanimbar, there was no such thing as neutrality.

That evening, Damianus came and escorted me to dinner. We walked through the village to his house, and Damianus invited me in and introduced me to his wife. Ibu Masele was a woman who neither spoke nor smiled. But she had a steady and forceful gaze that made me suspect that she was a woman who, like her husband, would not put up with much. She disappeared into the back of the house and reappeared a while later with some tea and biscuits.

'Have you brought a tape recorder?' Damianus asked.

I shook my head. 'No,' I said. It seemed presumptuous to turn up at somebody's house for a first visit with a tape recorder.

Before my arrival I had imagined that I would be spending my days in Tanimbar recording interviews, but I had found early on that the tape recorder spooked people. Some people refused to talk into it at all. Others became guarded, worried that their words might be later used against them. Other than doing duty as a low-quality music system for playing Tom Waits, the tape recorder remained almost entirely unused. But in Tumbur, it seemed, it was a necessary part of my armoury if I was to appear professional.

The sculptor scowled at me. 'If you are to do your research properly, you need a tape recorder,' he said.

'I have one, but it is still at the *pastoran*.'

'Go and fetch it,' Damianus said. 'I don't want to waste my breath.' He shooed me away with his hand.

I left Damianus's house and went back to the *pastoran* to get my tape player. I slotted in a new cassette, then headed back. When I arrived, I held it up for him to see. 'Got it,' I said.

'Good. Put it here.' Damianus tapped the tabletop.

I put the tape recorder down and pressed 'record'. Damianus started to talk. It was not a rehearsed script, but he was fluent and thoughtful, and as he spoke it was clear that his reflections on woodcarving had been honed by years of attention and discussion. Here was a man who was used to talking to outsiders about his art. He was a man who knew what he wanted to communicate and how he wanted to communicate it.

Damianus talked about the structure of the village *kelompoks*. Together, these work groups shared the monopoly on woodcarvings made for the tourist trade and for export. It was impossible to carve without being a member of one group or another – lone artists found themselves squeezed out of the market and ostracised. Being a member meant not only having your work audited for quality, but also being unable to sell below a certain minimum price, to avoid aggressive discounting and the kind of rush-to-the-bottom free-for-all that a free market might bring in its wake. The *kelompoks* not only set prices and negotiated bulk orders: they also were responsible for managing access to the precious *kayu hitam* out of which the sculptures were made. All of this was an extension of the traditional system – called *sasi*, and common throughout the province of Maluku – by which communities regulated access to resources.

Damianus talked for half an hour or so. The cassette player whirred softly. I drank tea and listened, interjecting occasionally.

'In Tumbur,' the sculptor concluded, 'we do not only sell sculptures like they do in other villages. That is what makes us great. We people in Tumbur don't just sell sculptures. We also sell history. If you buy a sculpture from another village, all you get is a piece of wood. It means nothing. It is different in Tumbur. When you buy a sculpture here, whether from me or from anyone else, what you take home to England is not only a sculpture. Do you see?'

I nodded. 'Yes,' I said. 'Selling history.'

'What you take back to England is a *story*,' Damianus said. 'It is a piece of our history. That is why people come here to buy our sculptures. For generations on end our ancestors have made sculptures here in Tumbur. Only here is there traditional art. That is why we are famous. Other places copy our sculptures. There are factories in Jakarta where they make copies of our work, but their sculptures are bad. They are not made out of *kayu hitam*. They do not know how to carve well. But, above all, they do not know our history. This means that the sculptures are worthless.'

Damianus went on. 'In other villages, they may try to cheat you. They will make *patung mandi* to cheat you.'

'*Patung mandi*?' I asked. *Bathroom carving*?

'They make a carving, then they put it in the *mandi*, the bathroom, where it is damp. They leave it for one, maybe two years until it looks ancient, and then they sell it to tourists as an antique. They pretend that it is old and sell it for a high price. But here in Tumbur, you have a living tradition. Here we do not do such things.'

Then Damianus smiled. He didn't smile often, and when he did, it was only briefly.

'Enough,' he said. 'Let us look at some sculptures and then we can eat.'

I switched off the tape and pressed 'rewind'. Damianus went out the back of the house and returned carrying a number of sculptures carved from *kayu hitam*. He placed them on the table. There were warriors, standing or squatting, brandishing swords and spears, holding the severed heads of their enemies. There were men with horns or head-dresses, holding their engorged cocks in their hands and staring into space. There were women unveiling their breasts or lifting their skirts. And they were all beautifully carved.

'This,' Damianus said, 'is our traditional Tanimbarese art.'

At that moment, his wife emerged from the back room with plates of noodles, fish, eggs and wilted vegetables.

'Let us eat,' Damianus said.

The sculptor and I ate together. His wife sat across the other side of the room, her shoulders slightly hunched, and watched. When we finished, she cleared away the plates.

'Tomorrow,' Damianus said, 'you must come here for breakfast. Come at seven, no later. We can talk some more. Don't forget your cassette recorder. But perhaps now you need to go and write about what I have said.'

I headed back to the *pastoran*.

After the complications of negotiating with Matias in Sera and with the ancestors in Alusi Krawain, things with Damianus appeared uncomplicated, free from ambiguity. My presence in Tumbur seemed to be neither a burden nor a matter that occasioned particular interest or discussion. It was simply another opportunity for Damianus to put across his point of view, another way that the sculptors of Tumbur could let the outside world know about their art. The transaction was simple, and in both of our interests: I wanted information, and information was what he wanted to give me. I was no longer stealing with the eyes. I was being marketed to. And in a way it was a relief, this straightforwardness, this sense that my interests were for once not overwhelmingly at odds with those of my hosts. The ancestors, *adat* complexities, moral ambiguities, all these were swept away. Here was a place I could do business, and it felt very strange indeed.

By the time I arrived back at the *pastoran*, the mosquitoes were beginning to bite. I went through the gate into the garden and unlocked the door, closing it behind me. Then I lit the oil lamp on the desk. The shadows on the lurid palm trees were strangely eerie in the flickering light of the hissing lamp.

The *pastoran* was just in front of a patch of marshy ground, and once I sat down at the desk to begin work, I noticed the continual background drone of swarming mosquitoes. One buzzed past my ear and, before I could swat it, I felt a sharp prick in the back of my neck. I slapped at my neck, and then rummaged in my bag for mosquito coils. I took out four, placing one on the ground at each corner of the desk, and I lit them. Sweet-smelling smoke began to fill the air. I settled back down, took out the cassette player and my notebook, opened up my Indonesian–English dictionary and started the painstaking business of transcribing my interview with Damianus. Up in the eaves, the gecko continued to call: *tok-eh, tok-eh, tok-eh*. Out of the corner of my eye I could see a spider making its slow way across the wall. I tried to focus on the task.

When the mosquito coils burned down, I lit new ones. Their effect was minimal. The mosquitoes seemed more or less untroubled by the smoke. They flew straight through and settled on my ankles and my bare feet, on my exposed arms, on the back of my neck. Then they feasted on my blood. I played fragments of the interview, re-wound, re-played, made notes and slapped at my exposed skin. It was exhausting. The mosquitoes made it hard to concentrate. I began to think more kindly of the spiders. Perhaps they would eat the mosquitoes. But they looked to me like they might prefer larger prey – moths, lizards or anthropologists.

Eventually I tired of the struggle with the insects and took refuge under the mosquito netting, rigging up some ineffectual patches to cover the holes. I turned out the light and lay there for a long time, scratching at my feet and ankles, listening to the buzz of mosquitoes, the rustle of the gecko in the roof and the scurry of the spiders.

15

HEARTS OF DARKNESS

I was woken soon after dawn by the crackle of a loudspeaker.

'Attention! Attention!'

I sat up in bed, startled. My arms, legs and feet were covered in bites.

'Attention! Attention!' came the voice again.

I clambered out of bed as the speakers crackled into life a third time.

'Work groups one, two and four, report to the church immediately. I repeat: work groups one, two and four, report to the church immediately,' said the voice.

I got up and had a quick wash. The mosquitoes had been busy in the night. I slathered antihistamine cream on the places where the clusters of bites were most livid and itchy, then I put on my clothes. Once dressed, I peered out of the door. The sun was up and the building site opposite was already busy. People were gathering with wheelbarrows, saws and trowels. Women with wicker baskets on their heads were laughing with each other. Old men were sitting in the shade of a broad tree, breaking stones with mallets. I could hear the steady *tok, tok, tok* as their mallets pounded on the stones.

I pulled my watch from my bag. It was eight in the morning, and I was late for breakfast with Damianus.

The loudspeaker continued to crackle and splutter. 'Attention! Attention! Could the following people please report to the church for duty immediately – those who fail to appear will be fined two thousand five hundred rupiah...'

I shut and locked the door of the *pastoran* behind me. When I opened the gate into the road, one of the women on the site called out something that I didn't understand, and everybody laughed. The *tok, tok, tok* of hammers stopped.

'Come and drink palm-wine!' called out one of the men on the site. He rose to his feet, grinning, beckoning me over.

I walked over to where he was standing. 'I haven't had breakfast yet,' I said. 'It's too early for palm-wine.'

He took hold of my upper arm, and squeezed it hard. 'Palm-wine will make you strong.'

'So will breakfast,' I said.

He passed me a full glass. I looked around the building site. Everybody had stopped working. They were all looking at me. I took the glass and downed it in a gulp.

He grinned. 'See,' he said, 'you already feel a little stronger.'

I wiped my mouth with my sleeve, then excused myself and headed down the road towards Damianus's house.

The loudspeaker was still blaring names. When I arrived, I found Damianus sitting on his porch with a microphone in hand, a pair of loudspeakers rigged up on his roof. I could hear the sound of a generator coming from behind the house. Damianus seemed to be enjoying himself. He grinned and waved at me and then – for my benefit, I suspected – he coughed and made a final announcement.

'Attention! Attention! Could the following people please report for duty...' Then he turned the microphone off, and put it back in its cradle. 'Hello,' he said. 'You are late.' He smiled. His smile was not without warmth.

I shrugged, and told him I'd overslept.

He indicated towards the microphone. 'It is for the church,' he said. 'The villagers must work hard to have it finished. We ask them to help with building the church. It is a religious duty, an act of devotion. It will be very beautiful when it is finished, full of fine sculpture.'

'Are they happy to work?'

'Some yes, some no. But we fine those who do not want to work. So everyone works, happy or not. It is much better like this. The church will be built more quickly.'

'How long will it take to complete?'

'Months, probably. Anyway, you must eat.'

Damianus ushered me into the house. I had brought my tape recorder with me, but when I took it out, he brushed it to one side, as if he hadn't the appetite for another speech. 'There is no need today' he said. 'Today we will just take it easy.'

His wife brought out sugar sandwiches – white bread and thick margarine, packed with large crystals of sugar – and hot tea sweet enough to set the teeth on edge. We spent the morning talking. Neighbours came to join in the conversation and then went away again. Sometimes Damianus interrupted our conversations to return to his microphone and to make further announcements about the construction work.

Damianus told me that he could make me a sculpture. He could offer me a good price, he said.

'The sculptures you saw yesterday are ordinary sculptures, but I am making some larger pieces that you might be interested in. If you like, I can give you a good price. You can take them back home with you, as evidence for your research.'

He went to the back of the house, and returned bringing two large half-finished sculptures, carved not from *kayu hitam* but from a softer, lighter wood.

'I am making several of these,' he said. 'Do you want a photograph?'

'Sure,' I said.

'Help me bring out the sculptures, then.'

There were ten of them in all. They were all beautifully fashioned, with horns and headdresses, and paired as male and female. Even though they were unfinished, Damianus's skill and delicacy were not in doubt.

We put the sculptures in a line outside Damianus's front door, making sure that the arrangement was symmetrical. Damianus took up his position behind the sculptures and posed with them. He did not smile for the camera. I took a single photograph.

Having done so, I pointed to the figures in the middle. 'Those are particularly beautiful,' I said.

'I'll finish those first,' he said, 'and you can take them away when you leave.' He offered me a price. The price was good. Damianus was a businessman, but he was fair minded in his dealings. We shook hands. Damianus seemed to approve of my choice, or at the very least knew how to flatter his customers.

'I think this pair are the best. This is a good choice.'

I stayed for lunch. The sculptor was in good spirits.

'However long you stay in Tumbur,' he said, 'you must come and eat with my family. We can talk, and you can learn. We will have the chance to relax and enjoy ourselves.'

I left after lunch. As I was heading back to the *pastoran*, I bumped into a man who was sitting on his doorstep, bunking off his duty in the church. He was carving a fine, sinuous sculpture out of wood. He had a conspiratorial air to him, and he called me over. He told me that he should have been breaking stones, but it was too hot and he preferred to sit in the shade, whittling away at *kayu hitam* with his penknife.

'Won't you get into trouble?' I asked him.

He shrugged. 'They will fine me,' he said, 'but I can make two sculptures in a day. The fine is the same as the money I get for one sculpture. So I make a profit. And if I don't get rich like this, at least here I can relax.' He grinned at me. 'Carving,' he said, 'is easy. Breaking stones is hard.'

Ӿ

Several days later, just when I was at risk of forgetting that I was in Tanimbar – with its *barang aneh*, its tales of ritual heat, its *adat* law and its ancestral powers – Damianus told me about the *walut* owned by his family.

'This *walut* is very powerful. It is a small one – we call them *luvu dalam* – and we keep it up in the eaves of the house. When the wind blows from the west, we place it in the eastern eaves, and when the wind blows from the east, we place it in the western eaves. Otherwise the heat from the sculpture would make the house hot, and we would get sick.'

Damianus told me that the sculpture was very *halus* – very fine – and that it was carved either from ivory or from the tooth of a dugong. Damianus said he suspected it was a dugong, although he was not sure. Once these small *walut* would have been used to protect warriors going to the battlefield. But the Catholic missions in Tanimbar had, from the very first, striven to redirect the passion for warfare into other pursuits, chiefly soccer. They were so successful in this that records show that, by the 1940s, in the northern Tanimbarese island of Larat there were already forty football teams.

'It is very useful, this sculpture,' Damianus told me. 'When we play the people of Atubul at football, we take my *walut*, and it is because of my *walut* that we win. The *walut* makes us powerful. Once we would bring it when our ancestors went to war. Now we use it for football.'

Although it was no longer used for protection in times of warfare, Damianus's *walut* was still a dangerous thing, and still held the power over both life and death. Some time ago, Damianus told me, as the Tumburese team was going out to play a match, they passed a well where a woman from Sangliat Dol was washing her face. A gust of wind took up the heat of the sculpture, the hot wind struck the woman and she immediately fell down dead. Her heart simply stopped beating.

When he got to the end of the story, Damianus smiled. 'Would you like to see the sculpture?' he asked.

'Yes, if you don't mind.'

Damianus said that he didn't mind. But he asked me to agree to one condition: that I write and sign a document, witnessed and counter-signed by at least three people, taking full responsibility for my actions.

'A document? You want me to sign a document?' I asked.

Damianus nodded. 'Yes. This is important. Then if you fall sick, or your plane crashes or you die, this is proof that we are not responsible, that it was your own choice to see the sculpture.'

'It the sculpture *that* dangerous?' I asked him.

Damianus shrugged. 'You Westerners do not believe these things, but we people in Tanimbar do believe. So the risk is your own. I cannot decide for you. My advice is that you should not take such a risk. But if your research is that important, and if you want to take the chance, then you can do so. We want a document for our own protection. If anything does happen to you, we want it to prove that it was not our fault.'

It felt like a test, although whether of discretion, delicacy or courage I was not sure. Either way, I decided to turn the offer down.

'I will take your advice,' I said.

Damianus seemed pleased with this. 'You are intelligent,' he said. 'Many foreigners are stupid, but it is better that you do not see the sculpture. As the head of the household, I can see it, and I will come to no harm. For anybody else it is dangerous.'

We talked more about *adat*. It turned out that Damianus had his own *kekuatan mata rumah*. He told me that he could take an ordinary chicken egg and prepare it with various hot herbs and roots. Then he could place it in the family cooking fire of his enemy, and his enemy's family would die, one by one.

He paused, to let the story sink in. Then he smiled and said, 'But I am a Christian man. I do not *main nakal*, I do not play around with bad things.'

✗

Over the next few days, I spent time getting to know people in the village, breaking stones with the men and women working on the church building site and drinking palm-wine, recording interviews with sculptors, spending time with Damianus and, in the evenings, sitting in my little house, swatting away the mosquitoes.

One morning, groggily shuddering awake as a particularly large spider scuttled in panic across my torso, I sat up and looked down at my feet. I started to count the red pinprick mosquito bites that covered them from toe to ankle. I stopped somewhere around one hundred, got up, slathered on a bit more cream to soothe the itching and went to have breakfast with Damianus. He was working on the two *walut*, the male and female figures, wielding his penknife with nonchalant skill. As I ate breakfast, he smoked and chatted gruffly about the stupidities of foreigners.

Later that day, Benny came to visit on his motorbike to see how I was getting on. It was good to see him. He had brought a small booklet that he said might interest me. It was simply titled *Patung*, meaning 'sculpture', and was compiled by the by the Dewan Kerajinan Propinsi Maluku (DKPM) – the Moluccan Provincial Committee for Handicrafts. I was aware of the DKPM. Damianus had mentioned them a few times. They were active in promoting the work of the sculptors of Tumbur. It was thanks to their efforts, in part, that the sculptures from this tiny village were well known in Ambon and beyond.

The booklet was a short guide for sculptors in Tumbur. On the first page was the title 'Observations and Instructions: Suggestions for Improvement of the Quality of Wood Carving Products in Tumbur Village, in the District of Tanimbar, South East Maluku'. The booklet explained, stage by stage, how traditional Tumburese artworks should be carved. The text recommended that sculptors concentrate on making 'figures resting their chins on one or two hands... figures with one or two horns... figures with the faces of beasts', and it went on to counsel that 'other forms in positions suggesting farming, fishing and dancing may be used, but emphasising postures that are unique to the area'. The booklet further suggested ideas that might go down well amongst tourists: headhunters with spears and swords, and carved wooden key fobs with severed heads at the end. There were also recommendations on the choice and conservation of wood, advice on setting prices (I noted I had got a very good price from Damianus for the two *walut* he had offered me) and warnings against making sculptures so elaborate that consumers would not be able to afford them.

But what struck me most were the curious little stick figures on the third page of the book, drawn with the finesse of graffiti on the wall of a public toilet, depicting sculptures of male and female figures. I read the caption: 'Differences in the sexes of sculptures should be made explicit. The sexual organs should not be seen as shameful or pornographic.'

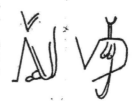

3. Perbedaan bentuk anatomis patung pria dan Wanita harus jelas. Alat kelamin tidak harus dianggap sebagai hal yang porno atau tidak wajar.

I pointed to the pictures. 'What's all this about?' I asked Benny.

He shrugged. 'These are traditional sculptures,' he said. 'They are *primitif*.'

I thought of the Frenchman on his strange quest for real, authentic savages. I thought of the catalogue of dubious intentions that made up the history of anthropology. And I wondered whether the sculptors of Tumbur were truly selling their own history, or whether they were selling instead a history dreamed by others – a history dreamed by outsiders.

Ϫ

For these outsiders, Tanimbar, like many other places, has always functioned as a kind of primitive 'elsewhere', a place on which to project dreams and fantasies and imaginings. Sex and death – it is always about one or the other. Or sometimes both.

Long after I returned from Tanimbar, I came across a copy of a French comic book, published in 1969. The comic was *Akim*, a rip-off of the Tarzan franchise, which started life in Italy, and then went on to success in France. Issue 247 is called 'La Prison de Tanimbar', but the cover depicts a scene so very unlike the actual Tanimbar that it takes some unpicking to work out what exactly is going on.

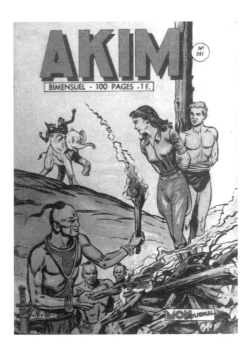

The opening pages go some way to explaining what is happening. The story is an adolescent boy's fever dream, with death, betrayal and a sexy-but-cruel queen called Samara. Akim, the hero of the series, has been separated from his animal sidekicks by Samara, and brought under her spell. Here is how the story begins:

> Desiring to reconquer at any price the kingdom of Tanimbar, from where she has been driven, Samara, the cruel queen of the tigers, has struck Akim with an arrow coated with a drug that makes him blindly obey her orders. As a result the animals that could resist Samara's plans have all been driven out into the forest, and Rita and Jim have been exiled on a lost island in the centre of a volcano... Akim, Samara and an expeditionary force of one hundred elite warriors trained by Akim embark for Tanimbar, just as Jim and Rita manage to escape [from the volcano] and also arrive [in Tanimbar]. Rita just has the time to fire in Akim's direction an arrow which would inject him with a substance that could snatch him from out of Samara's grip, but then she too is captured, along with Jim, by the Maladan warriors.

I have no idea where the authors of *Akim* got the name Tanimbar. There is no village called Maladan in Tanimbar, nor has there ever been (although there is, confusingly, a small settlement near Yogyakarta on Java called Maladan). And everything about the story and setting in *Akim* is wrong: the Maladan warriors do not look Tanimbarese; there are no elephants or tigers on Tanimbar; and Tanimbar has never known any cruel-but-sexy warrior-queens, even if the warrior prowess of Atuf's sibling, Inkelu, came close.

Whilst reading *Akim*, it is not even clear where on the planet the Tanimbar of this story is situated – whether in Indonesia or elsewhere. 'Tanimbar', in other words, is simply used as a shorthand for 'some-where exotic'. It is a place where people with names like Jim and Rita could have adventures amongst savages and warrior-queens. I wondered whether the frustrated Frenchman I met in Saumlaki had read 'La Prison de Tanimbar' as a child. No wonder he was disappointed.

𐤉

Anthropologists are not immune to fantasies of the exotic, even if anthropology has a hard time owning up to that fact. As I look back to my own time spent amongst the *barang aneh* of the Tanimbar Islands, I can't help but see the tales that I am weaving here as being continuous with the stories in publications like *Akim* – dubious accounts of colonial derring-do, tales of Europeans finding themselves amongst savage customs and rites. I, too, am guilty. And recognising the fact does not diminish my guilt. Perhaps it augments it.

𐤉

One day in Tumbur, I was sitting on the beach, talking to a group of men. Some of the men were from Tumbur, others were from nearby villages. We were talking about Westerners who had passed through the islands when a man from Arui Bab told me about an American anthropologist who had visited Tanimbar. She was, he said, a dedicated and brilliant scholar, and she came in search of knowledge.

'For science,' he said. 'She came for science.'

As for her subject matter, she was committed to understanding the sexual prowess of the primitive races. And because she was a good scientist, she needed to *experience* this prowess first-hand.

The other men on the beach all nodded and murmured approval.

The American scholar came to Tanimbar, and made some preliminary investigations. She asked around, she visited several villages. But, the man from Arui Bab told me, she was disappointed by what she found. The people of Tanimbar were simply not primitive enough. So after a few weeks, she left in the direction of Irian Jaya – that world of penis sheaths, cassowaries and pig hunts – to track down a husband with a real, live heart of darkness.

'Is this true?' I asked.

'Of course,' he said. 'Many people know this.'

The other men all nodded wisely.

'You are not joking?' I asked.

'Why would we joke about these things?' the man from Arui Bab asked me. 'These things are serious.'

I have since done my best to find a trace of this mysterious anthropologist. Perhaps she disappeared for good in Irian Jaya. Perhaps she never existed at all. Or perhaps, having enjoyed two exhausting years of participant penetration as the bride of a tribal chieftain in a remote, mist-shrouded valley, she is now back in America, settled down on some quiet university campus, where she spends her days preparing her monograph on savage sexual practices.

'But is this *really* true?' I persisted.

The man from Arui Bab shrugged and looked out to sea. 'Yes, it is true,' he said. 'People who I have talked to about this admire this woman. They say that she did all this for science. She did all this for a book. This is a great self-sacrifice.'

The other men murmured in agreement. We sat together, looking out to sea, pondering the anthropologist's self-martyrdom.

Ӿ

Damianus had been carving since childhood. He owed his skill and knowledge to the shadowy Herman de Vries, of whom Matias had also spoken. De Vries was a Dutch lay worker for the Catholic church. He worked as a carpenter in the Catholic mission in Ambon and then, during the 1950s, he moved to Merauke in Western New Guinea, where he was a community worker alongside the anthropologist-priest Petrus Drabbe. Perhaps through Drabbe's influence, after his retirement from his official duties some time around 1970, de Vries arrived in Tanimbar.

If the twentieth century was ruinous for the rich cultural heritage of the Tanimbarese, this was so largely on account of the Catholic and Protestant missionaries. Early in the century the Protestants, in the fervour of iconoclastic piety, consigned countless figures carved of wood, ivory and bone to the flames, so that the Tanimbarese might put their idolatry behind them. More subtle than their Protestant counterparts, the Catholics preferred instead to remove objects – often in exchange for derisory gifts such as small amounts of tobacco – and ship them away to be held in museums.

If the first wave of cultural destruction in Tanimbar was on account of the pieties of the missionaries, the second was caused by the global trade in 'primitive' art that took off after the Second World War. As so-called primitive art rose in value, so did the pace of collecting. This suited the missions perfectly, and the commercial demands of the art market went hand in hand with the fervour of the Churches, eager to see the people of Tanimbar put their old beliefs behind them.

It was in this context that de Vries came to Tanimbar. When he arrived, he set about buying up as many traditional artworks as he could. He bought sculptures, carvings and heirloom gold. In one village, they told me, he chiselled away stone figures that had sat for generations at the bottom of the village steps leading down to the beach. He took them away for sale. Other people told me that he bought up old *tavu* or house-altars, *kora ulu* or prow boards, or little *walut* sculptures. Some of the sculptures can now be found in the musée du quai Branly in Paris. And the strange thing was this: in all of this frenzy of purchasing, de Vries seemed to be curiously exempt from the rage of the ancestors.

Perhaps he was lucky, or perhaps the Catholic God somehow trumped the ancestors' power.

I had heard de Vries' name several times in Tanimbar. He always seemed to be a curiously ambiguous figure. He gave Matias a livelihood. Abraham, too, had met him: the Dutch carpenter had shown the sculptor from Alusi Krawain images from Petrus Drabbe's ethnography, so that he might emulate them. But it was in Tumbur that de Vries had the biggest impact, because there he not only bought sculptures, but also actively encouraged a whole carving industry. As one man said, 'de Vries bought all the sculptures that there were to buy, and when there were no more sculptures, he taught us how to make them, so he could keep buying.' De Vries brought to Tumbur folders full of photostats of sculptures to act as templates. Damianus was direct. 'It was de Vries who started everything,' he said. 'This was back in 1971, when we were still at school. He showed us how to carve. He gave us pictures and told us to copy them.'

The four sculptors de Vries trained – Samuel Nerenere, Xaverius Sainyakit, Martinus Nerenere and Damianus himself – were all children at the time. Later they became the heads of the village *kelompoks*. Now, almost a quarter of a century on, the industry provided employment for one hundred men. It was thanks to de Vries and to the woodcarving industry he initiated that Tumbur was the most prosperous of all Tanimbarese villages.

And yet, something sat uncomfortably with me. One day I asked Damianus if he had any of the photocopies that de Vries had shown him. The sculptor looked at me steadily, and told me that they had all been thrown away. They were low quality, he said. They had been useful when the sculptors were learning how to carve. But now that they were skilled at working in wood, they no longer had any use for them.

X

I wondered about those photocopies. Something about the sculptures from the village of Tumbur was nagging at me, and I was not sure precisely what. They seemed strangely familiar in a way I could not quite pin down.

Then, one night as I was sitting and working in the *pastoran*, swatting away the mosquitos, it came to me. I remembered the suburban homes in England, back when I was growing up in the 1970s and 1980s; I recalled mantelpieces adorned with Maasai carvings of warriors, delicately fashioned from black ebony – sculptures made for a tourist market hungry for primitive art, strange kin to the *kayu hitam* sculptures of Tumbur. In my childhood, those Maasai sculptures were almost paradigms for the Western fantasy of 'primitive' art. Whatever else de Vries was or wasn't, he was clearly an astute businessman. He knew what would sell and what wouldn't. And the thought that the sculptures of Tumbur might possibly have had their ancestry not in the Tanimbarese past, but instead in the tourist art of Africa, was a queasy one.

There is now no way of telling, of course. All of this is too far in the past. The photostats have long been destroyed, and Herman de Vries is no more. But it was hard to rid myself of the suspicion that the art of the Tumburese had a genealogy more complex and tangled than it first appeared.

16

MIRROR IMAGES

Several days into my stay in Tumbur, another foreigner turned up. The first I heard of him was when somebody came running into Damianus's house to say that an *orang bule* had arrived in the village.

The foreigner was so large it was terrifying, the messenger said. And he was bleeding copiously. '*Tuan*,' the messenger pleaded with me, 'the foreigner doesn't speak any Indonesian. Please come and translate. We are afraid of him.'

Damianus nodded to me. 'Go and see,' he said.

I walked out of the house and down to the main street. There I saw an enormous pale foreigner, dressed in shorts, pushing a motorbike, with a large camera dangling around his neck. Blood was pouring down his right leg.

I recognised him immediately. He was a Dutch journalist. We had met a week or so before in Saumlaki. We had run into each other in the main street, and shared a coffee in the Harapan Indah, where he was staying. The Dutchman was on a journalistic assignment from a youth magazine in the Netherlands; he had been commissioned to write a piece on the sculpture of Tumbur. He was affable and interested, but not enormously well informed. I had been expecting him to turn up in the village before too long, but not in this abject state.

I went over to make sure that he was not too badly hurt. The journalist looked embarrassed. He had borrowed the motorbike from Pastor Böhm, but had taken a fall just outside Tumbur. Although he had not broken anything, there was a large bloody gash below his right knee.

'I don't think it is serious,' he said, 'but I've dented the motorbike.'

It was not the most auspicious entrance. And, certainly, the people of the village were not fully equipped to deal with a man of such dimensions, pouring blood from his shin and unable to communicate in Indonesian. So I took charge, and led him back to Damianus's house where he cleaned himself up and washed his wound. We found some more-or-less clean cloth to act as a bandage. By the time the Dutch journalist's bleeding leg was bound and trussed, a small crowd had gathered to look at the new arrival. Ibu Masele brought tea for everyone.

Damianus looked at me, and then, in Indonesian, he asked me, 'Who is the fat man?'

'He's a journalist,' I said.

'He doesn't speak Indonesian?'

'No.'

Damianus grunted. 'I don't like him,' he said. 'Is he a friend of yours?'

'I've seen him before, in Saumlaki. We had a coffee, but that was the first time we'd met.'

'Why is he here?'

'He's interested in sculpture. He has come to take photographs.'

'I don't like him,' Damianus repeated.

I paused. 'What do you want me to do? Shall I tell him to go away?'

Damianus shrugged. 'Ask him what he wants.'

'Okay.'

The Dutchman was sipping his tea, smiling at both Damianus and me with an expression of anxious good will. 'This is Damianus,' I said. 'He wants to know why you are here.'

The Dutchman smiled at Damianus. 'Tell him I have come to find out about how they make sculpture in the village.'

I translated this into Indonesian. Damianus scowled. 'Does the fat journalist know anything about Tumbur, or is he ignorant?'

'Do you know much about Tumbur?' I asked.

The journalist smiled. 'Pastor Böhm gave me a copy of Drabbe's book. I read some of it yesterday. I've seen some sculptures.'

I rendered this into Indonesian. Damianus spread his hands wide. 'What does he want from me?'

'Damianus would like to know what he can do to help you?' I said. It did not take much linguistic skill to infer the difference in tone between Damianus's weary bad temper and my own polite request.

The Dutchman unslung his camera from around his neck. 'I need photographs,' he said. 'I am writing an article for a magazine for children and young people, so I'd like some pictures of children learning to make sculptures.'

I relayed this to Damianus.

'We don't teach children here,' Damianus explained. 'They just make sculptures of their own accord.'

The journalist frowned. 'But I want to see how children learn here. Ask him if I can photograph him with some children, making sculptures.'

When I explained this to him, Damianus laughed. 'This man is an idiot,' he said. 'He knows nothing.'

'What's he saying?' asked the journalist.

'We're talking about the photographs,' I said. 'Wait a second.' I negotiated with Damianus a few moments more, doing my best to make the case for the Dutch journalist. The Dutchman seemed frustrated to be excluded from the conversation, and so he butted in.

'What is "children" in Indonesian?' he asked.

'*Anak-anak*,' I said.

'*Anak-anak*,' the journalist said to Damianus.

Damianus sighed. 'If he wants photographs of children, he must give me cigarette money. If he gives me some money for cigarettes, he can have his photographs.'

'He wants some money for cigarettes if you are to take some photos,' I translated.

'No problem,' the journalist smiled, and then returned to Damianus and said again, '*Anak-anak*?'

Damianus nodded. 'Let's take the photographs first, then he can buy me cigarettes.'

The sculptor and some of his neighbours rounded up a number of children to be photographed. The children laughed and jostled as the journalist herded them into an aesthetic grouping.

'Go over there!' he said. 'No, not there, but there! Good! Well done! Could I have another child over here? Look, can you translate for me? That child, over there. Good. Okay. One more child. Can we find one more child?'

I translated the photographer's directions as he manhandled several children into position.

'He's so fat!' the children giggled. 'He's so fat and white!'

The photographer turned his attention to Damianus. 'Now, ask the sculptor – what is his name again? – to join them. I want him to stand behind them.'

'Damianus,' I said, 'the Dutchman wants you to be in the photograph as well. He wants you to look as if you are teaching them.'

'I'm not a teacher, I'm a sculptor,' Damianus said.

'I'm only translating his words,' I reminded him. 'I'm not saying what you should do.'

The sculptor seemed to accept this. 'Okay,' he said. 'But he better give me some decent money for cigarettes.' He went to join the group.

Seeing the sculptor standing there for the photo, I felt guilty, an accomplice to something in which I'd rather not be involved. *Curi mata*. Stealing with the eyes, once again.

The Dutchman adjusted his light meter. He took a couple of test shots. 'Now, tell the sculptor to sit down and put a child on his knee,' he said.

'Damianus,' I said, 'he wants you to sit down with a child on your knee.'

'Idiot,' Damianus growled, sitting down on a log. He pulled a child onto his lap, and picked up a sculpture and a knife. 'Is this what he wants?' he asked.

'I think so,' I said.

The photographer was smiling. 'Now get him to give the sculpture to the child, and ask him to point,' he said.

I translated.

'But this is a lie,' Damianus said, handing the child the sculpture. 'We do not teach children like this. They just watch and learn.'

The guilt burned a little more. 'If you want, I can tell him to go away,' I said. 'You don't have to do what he asks.'

Damianus shrugged. Then he pointed at the sculpture, pretending to teach, and scowled.

'Thank you,' said the journalist. He spent the next couple of minutes snapping photographs. Finally, he put his lens cap back on. 'Thank you,' he said to Damianus. The journalist turned to face me, 'Thank you. I really appreciate your help. I think it will be a good article.'

'I hope so,' I replied. 'But I think that Damianus isn't happy, so I suggest you get him some cigarettes.'

'Where do I get cigarettes?'

'There's a small shop down the road. I'll show you where.'

I pointed the way and the journalist limped off. The children dispersed.

Damianus swore under his breath, and I apologised to him.

A few moments later the journalist returned with a packet of cigarettes. 'Only one packet, after all that trouble?' Damianus was incredulous. 'You would think that from the money he will make out of his article, he could have bought a case of ten.'

This was entirely my fault. I knew the etiquette, and the journalist didn't. A single packet of cigarettes was a derisory gift. Damianus grabbed the cigarettes from the journalist without thanking him.

The journalist rubbed his hands together. 'Okay,' he said, 'I have to go.'

Damianus was brooding. 'He should drink palm-wine with us,' the sculptor said.

This was a subtle suggestion on Daminaus's part. It had been a difficult meeting, but if there is anything that can mend broken relationships, it is palm-wine.

'He also wants you to get palm-wine,' I said. 'Go back to the shop and get him some. Stay and drink palm-wine. It will help smooth things over.'

'What's the Indonesian for palm-wine?' the journalist asked.

'*Sopi*,' I said.

'Okay,' he said. 'I'll be back soon.'

When he returned, Damianus's wife brought out a glass. Damianus filled a glass for each guest in turn. One by one we downed the palm-wine, passing the glass back to the sculptor to be refilled. The ceremony had all the seriousness of a sacrament, and as far as Damianus was concerned, this was exactly what it was. Palm-wine, he was to say later, is a sacred drink.

'We have to drink from the same glass?' the Dutchman protested. 'Isn't that unhygienic?'

'The palm-wine will kill everything,' I said. 'Us included.'

'I can't get drunk. I'll come off my bike again.'

'Drink a little and pour the rest onto the floor,' I reassured him. 'The important thing is to be seen to drink something and to hand the glass back empty.'

The Dutchman took a sip, then poured the palm-wine out onto the ground. He passed the glass back to Damianus.

'He doesn't drink much,' the sculptor said. He poured another glass and passed it on.

As soon as he possibly could, before the palm-wine began its second round, the Dutchman made his excuses and left, mounting his motorbike and riding out of the village back to Saumlaki.

✗

When the palm-wine was finished, I too left. I didn't feel like heading back to the *pastoran* and the gloomy company of the spiders, so instead I walked down to the beach. I would be leaving Tumbur in a few days' time. After Tumbur, I did not have many other plans in Tanimbar. My time there felt as if it were coming to an end. I sat by the shore and watched the waves roll in, thinking about Tanimbar, wondering if, once I left, I would ever come back, and when that might be.

As I was sitting there, a group of villagers appeared and joined me. A couple of them I knew by sight. One of them had been introduced to me a couple of days before as 'the Murderer'. He wore grubby white shorts and fake aviator shades. He had done time in Ambon for killing a neighbour, his friend had told me, but he was unrepentant. When his friend had said this, the Murderer had smiled.

Along with the Murderer was a man I knew by sight from my conversations at the building site opposite the *pastoran*. There were another couple of younger men who I didn't recognise, and two women. One of the women was strikingly attractive. She told me that she had lost her husband in an accident a year or two before. She asked me if I was married. I said that I wasn't.

'You are all alone here without a wife,' she teased. 'You must be lonely.'

The villagers all laughed. The Murderer laughed longer than all the others.

'I'm fine,' I said. 'I have my work to keep me busy.'

'You should be careful,' she said. 'Tonight I'll climb in through the window of the *pastoran* and I'll fuck you until it hurts.'

She punched my arm and let out a long, hard laugh. The other villagers joined in the laughter. The Murderer's glasses glinted in the afternoon sun. The widow dug me in the ribs with her elbow.

For some reason – perhaps it was nervousness, perhaps it was the palm-wine – I too found this incredibly funny. So, as the sea rolled in, we sat there on the sand and we laughed. And then, when we'd finished laughing, I shook their hands and wished them well.

I headed back to the *pastoran*. 'Remember,' the widow called after me, 'until it hurts!'

That evening, when I turned up for dinner, Damianus had recovered enough of his presence of mind to joke about the Dutchman.

'Do you have many visitors like him?' I asked the sculptor.

'Far too many,' he said. 'But it is good publicity for us, even if it is all lies. Even lies are good publicity. They mean that we can sell more sculptures. They mean more people come here to Tumbur, and perhaps when they come here, if they stay long enough, they will see what are lies and what is true.'

Damianus's wife came in and silently served us noodles and stewed vegetables.

'There is a film tonight,' said Damianus, 'in the headman's house. I think you should come.'

'A film?'

Damianus shrugged. 'Someone has gone into Saumlaki on a motor-bike to choose it. Kung-fu, something like that.'

It sounded preferable to another evening of solitude in the *pastoran*. Besides, I was tired of making notes and transcribing cassettes. I told Damianus that I would see him there.

When I arrived at the headman's house, the room was already full. The television was on, a grey fuzz in the corner, and a young man fiddled with the video player. I could hear the sound of a generator out the back.

There was no space to sit, but when I came in, someone cuffed the ear of a child sitting in a chair, and indicated that I should take the child's place. Damianus was not yet there, but the room was already crammed. Women sat on the floor, staring at the grey blizzard on the screen, wide eyed with expectation as they breastfed their children. Old men sat at the back smoking clove cigarettes, their skinny legs crossed. Clusters of children crowded in wherever they could.

As I sat down, the man next to me whispered in my ear, 'We are showing an English film. I think you will like it.'

Some time after, the screen flickered into life. A rustle of anticipation swept through the room. A familiar tune started up, and then an even more familiar voice.

'Pretty woman...' sang Roy Orbison.

On the screen I could see the heights of Rio de Janeiro. Christ's arms opened wide over the city. Roy continued to croon.

'Is that London?' the man next to me asked.

'No, it's Rio de Janeiro,' I told him.

He thought about this. 'London is very beautiful,' he said.

I was about to correct him when my attention was drawn back to the screen by a startling sight. The scene had cut to a sun-drenched villa, and there against the wall was a sultry model in the most nominal of red bikinis. The colour control of the television had been turned up so that her tiny swimsuit glowed with an unnatural, pulsing intensity. The men in the room leaned forward. The woman in the bikini writhed against the wall, playing with her hair, sucking her fingers.

'Daaarling can't you see...?' pleaded Roy.

'Western women are frightening,' my neighbour confided. 'We are afraid that when more tourists come to Tanimbar, then women like this will come.'

'You are afraid?' The atmosphere in the headman's house was not quite one of fear.

'Yes, we are afraid.' he said. 'It's all right for you. You come from the West. You know how to cope with women like that. But for us here in Tanimbar it is frightening.'

Another man turned to me. 'The government want to turn Tumbur into a tourist village,' he said. 'They want to build a swimming pool so that lots of Westerners will come. There will be women dressed like that, in bikinis. They will want to have sex with us. This makes us afraid.'

'Is it true that in the West people can have sex with whoever they like?' another man asked. 'When we watch films from the West, we see that everybody has sex all the time and everybody carries a gun. We don't want Tumbur to become like the West. Our village is peaceful and calm. We are scared of the future.'

Then a man stood up and abruptly turned off the video. There was a sigh of disappointment. 'We have another film,' he announced.

'That woman is too frightening,' my neighbour whispered. 'We cannot bear to look at her.' In the dark, I could not tell if he was serious. The man by the video recorder fiddled around for a while, and put another tape in the video recorder.

My next-door neighbour touched me on the arm. 'Action film,' he said.

There was the sound of gunfire. The screen went black. From out of the darkness emerged Arnold Schwarzenegger's obscenely grinning face, exulting in his latest kill.

'Guns,' my neighbour said. 'There are so many guns in the West.'

'I'm tired,' I whispered. 'I think I'll go to bed.'

I left the headman's house and walked away through the village until I could no longer hear the sound of gunfire. Crickets were purring. The occasional fruit bat flew overhead, big and slow. The moon was large in the sky.

Ϫ

Back in the *pastoran*, I glanced at my watch and saw that it was still early. I had some interviews to transcribe – it was slow and boring work, but I thought I might as well plough on, to spare myself later. I left the door open to let in the night breezes, lit four mosquito coils around my feet and, shrouded in a cloud of pungent smoke, set to work. The mosquitoes flew through the smokescreen without a shudder.

After an hour or so, there was a knock on the open door. 'Excuse me,' said the man outside politely. 'Can I talk to you?'

I was relieved by the break. 'Come in,' I said. 'Sit down.' It was nine in the evening.

My guest sat down, introducing himself as Markus. 'I am a sculptor,' he said. 'I have been living in Tumbur all my life, and I have made sculpture since I was small. But I am worried about what will happen to us here in Tumbur.'

'Why should you be worried?' I asked.

'Soon there will be no wood,' he said. 'Last month a man from the logging company came. We are afraid he will cut down the trees. When we have no more trees there will be no more sculptures. We will not have money to buy food to eat. This is not the first time.'

'What do you mean?'

'Three years ago there was another logging company in Tumbur. We told them to leave. We tried to protest. We have the right to this land. These trees are our trees; they are our ancestors' trees. So, when the logging company didn't leave, we burnt down their houses and their headquarters. Then the military police came. They started shooting at us. We ran into the forest and hid. Three hundred people were arrested.

Many were beaten. They took us to jails in Ambon and in Kei. We make jokes about the jail as a government hotel. Five star, we said. I was held in the government hotel in Kei. I got very sick. I have only got back recently.'

I was not sure what to say.

'Now I am back,' Markus continued, 'another company has come to cut down our trees. They are buying sculptures because they want us to trust them. They say it is *kemajuan* – they say that it is progress. They say that they will build houses and roads. But when the forests are gone, we will be finished. When the forests are gone, the topsoil will wash away. When the forests are gone, Tanimbar will die.'

Markus stood up to leave. 'I just came to tell you this,' he said. 'You should know these things about Tanimbar. It is good that people know these things.'

I walked him to the door and shook his hand. Standing in the doorway of the *pastoran*, I watched him walk off into the village.

I closed the door and returned to my notes and my tapes.

That night I slept badly. I lay in bed listening for the sound of the widow who said she would climb through the window and fuck me till it hurt. I thought about Markus in his government hotel. I thought about the Dutchman, his photographs and his bloodied leg. And when I slept, I dreamed of Roy Orbison, of Arnold Schwarzenegger, of police out in the forest with their guns, of women in red bikinis sucking at their fingers, and of Christ with his arms wide open over the city of Rio.

Sex and death. Death and sex. Tanimbarese dreams of the West, and Western dreams of Tanimbar. The two were almost-perfect mirror images.

PART V

MANDI ADAT

RITUAL LAW BATHING

Sculpture by Damianus Masele, Department of
Anthropology collection, Durham University

17

ARRIVAL AND DEPARTURE

A few days later, Damianus finished the carvings: a male and female *walut*. They were lovely sculptures. I paid Damianus for the sculptures and ate lunch with him a final time. I was grateful for the straightfor-wardness of the transaction. He was in expansive mood, relaxed and good humoured. After lunch he carefully packed the sculptures with cardboard and dried grass, so that they were safe to transport. He was a professional. He knew what he was doing. When I wished him farewell, his wife also came out and said goodbye.

I shook her hand, and for the first time since meeting her, she smiled. 'Goodbye,' she said.

Benny came to pick me up on his motorbike.

'How have things gone?' he asked.

'Good,' I said. 'Very different from anywhere else in Tanimbar.'

Benny laughed. 'Yes,' he said. 'Here in Tumbur, people are organised.'

I packed my bags and we loaded up the motorbike. As I locked the door behind me, I felt strangely sad to be leaving the *pastoran* for the final time.

Benny started the engine. I could still hear the *tok, tok, tok* of the building site. A couple of villagers looked up and waved me goodbye. We headed back down the road to Saumlaki.

Ӿ

On returning to Saumlaki, I found the town in a state of excited antici-pation. The diocese of Amboina had a new bishop. He was taking over from his Dutch predecessor, and came from Menado. This made him the first Indonesian bishop of Amboina, and he was about to make his first visit to the Tanimbar Islands. The Catholics – by far the majority in Saumlaki – were out in force preparing for the arrival, whilst the Protes-tants were affecting looks of exaggerated indifference.

In the street in Olilit Baru, I came across a groups of women rehears-ing traditional dances, their arms out like frigate birds, dancing like Atuf and Inkelu danced at the dawn of time. Further down the road in Saumlaki, there was the shrill warbling of a flute orchestra. When I arrived back home, I found that Ibu Neli, a skilled composer, was writing a welcome song.

She sang it to me in her soft, quiet voice. The melody was simple and beautiful.

'It sounds good,' I said. 'I am sure the bishop will like it.'

I stopped by the airline office in the Harapan Indah and booked a ticket back to Ambon. The flight was scheduled to leave a few days after the arrival of the new bishop. My work in Tanimbar was almost done. I had no other leads to follow up, and I had plenty of material to work on. Besides, I was running out of money, and I needed to get home and find myself a job. My reserves were at an end.

I set to work on my final report for the Indonesian Institute of Sci-ences, typing out my thoughts on sheets of yellowed foolscap. I still have a copy of the report. The front page reads:

Draft final report on research project
Surat Izin Penelitian No. 5854/I/KS/1994
and No. 639/II.2.05/Ap/1995 (issued Ambon).
Kerjasama dgn. Universitas Pattimura, Ambon.
Oktober 1994–Maret 1995.

I was not sure anybody was ever going to read it. But it felt substantial and important, and as I laid down line after line of detached academic prose, I could sustain the illusion that my research – this strange exercise in stealing with the eyes – had not been entirely in vain. It felt good to gain some control over the havoc of impressions and experiences of the past few months. Writing it felt like a justification of my presence in Tanimbar. The measured prose gave me the impression of having tied up loose ends, as if I knew what I was about. When I read the report now, almost a quarter of a century later, I am surprised by how *cool* it seems, how distanced and reasonable. It reads like a piece of work written by somebody in full control of their faculties. There is none of the turbulence, sickness and confusion that I remember most from those long, strange months.

I was conscious that I would not be much longer in Tanimbar, so I spent my free time seeing friends, or walking through the Yamdena Plaza and down the jetty to look out across the bay. For those few days, I felt unexpectedly and deeply contented. Tanimbar seemed a different place to the town where I had landed several months before. I had come to like it. I had no regrets about my relationship with Damianus. To some extent, this compensated for the difficulties I had experienced with Matias and Abraham. And the coming episcopal visitation gave the town a carnival air. There were dancers and flute players rehearsing everywhere.

One day, I took a break from writing and went to call on Pastor Böhm. He was as hospitable as ever, but he had the air of a man deeply preoccupied. I didn't stay long. He probably had more important things to worry about than my research.

On the morning of the bishop's arrival, Benny called to accompany me to the airport. The bishop was due to arrive on the flight from Ambon at ten o' clock in the morning. Saumlaki was rammed full of people who had come down from the villages to join the welcoming party. In the main street was the vehicle that had been prepared to convey the bishop from the airport to the church in Olilit Baru, where he was to give his first address to the Tanimbarese. It was a small Suzuki truck, ornamented with painted hardboard flourishes that, with a certain amount of imagination, made it look like a traditional Tanimbarese war canoe. There was a platform at the back where the bishop was to stand and bless the crowds as he went in procession through the town. Unfortunately, it had run into difficulties: the hardboard decorations were so elaborate that the vehicle could not pass underneath the electricity wires without danger of electrocution. Young men were shinning up the pylons as if they were coconut palms, hitching up the low-slung wires to allow the truck to pass. Before long, the bishop's ceremonial conveyance shuddered off toward the airport, garlanded with brightly coloured bunting.

Benny and I caught a lift to the airport with Suster Astrid. The Catholic sisters had hired a minibus, and they were excited. Loud music blared from the stereo in the front of the bus. Suster Astrid slapped her thighs and sang along.

'We're going to see the bishop! We're going to see the bishop!'

The nuns whooped and giggled. We tore up the road to the airport at speed, dodging potholes.

Suster Astrid shook the driver's arm. 'Faster!' she urged him. 'Faster!'

I pulled a look of fear, only half in jest.

The nun gave a delighted grin. 'William is afraid of Tanimbarese driving!' she sang, pinching me hard on the arm. 'He's afraid! He's afraid! He's afraid!' After all, what was there to fear? Who could possibly crash on a day as auspicious as this?

The airport jostled with excited crowds even more than the main street. Two young women from Olilit Baru, dressed extravagantly in traditional clothing – gold heirlooms hanging from their ears and around their necks, stuffed birds of paradise in their hair – were preparing to garland the bishop with traditional ikat cloths. The *adat* chief of Olilit Baru had reached a compromise between traditional and modern dress. He wore Western trousers – for who would greet a bishop in a loincloth? – and a smart Western-cut ikat jacket. Around his head he wrapped another ikat, once again topped with a bird of paradise.

Schoolchildren were everywhere. The Catholic schools had pronounced the day a holiday, a day of compulsory celebration. Kids ran around in their blue-and-white uniforms, playing tag amongst the crowd. A couple of Western tourists wandered about as well, waiting for the plane back to Ambon, bewildered to be caught up in the hubbub.

Two troupes of rival musicians from the neighbouring villages of Wowonda and Ilngei, armed with bamboo flutes and drums, were waiting to make their musical offerings. They were dressed smartly, one group in matching blue-and-white baseball caps, the other spotlessly turned out in white shirts and brown trousers. Pastor Böhm was waiting to greet his new superior. His long white cassock shone brilliantly in the morning sun. On his face was a look of gravitas entirely appropriate to the occasion.

The plane from Ambon appeared through a bank of cloud. People pointed upwards excitedly as it turned on its course for descent. The small twin-prop growled its way bad temperedly down to the runway and disappeared out of sight behind the palm trees. It turned at the end of the runway and reappeared to taxi to a halt in front of the expectant masses.

The schoolteachers rounded up the children and chided them into silence.

The door of the plane opened.

A hush fell upon the crowd.

Pastor Böhm walked across the tarmac with long, decisive strides. The two bands started up, playing rival military marches, the flutes shrilling out of tune. And, in the doorway of the plane, dressed in white with splashes of Episcopal purple, appeared the bishop.

The bishop gave a little wave and a broad, buck-toothed grin. He started to descend the steps.

The woman in front of me, breaking the silence, muttered to her friend, 'But he is tiny!', and then she collapsed into irreverent giggles.

She was right. The bishop could not have been much more than five feet tall. As he grinned and waved on the tarmac, I could feel a slight shudder of disappointment go through the crowd. He didn't *look* that imposing. But then somebody started to cheer, and the cheer spread through the crowd, and everything was all right again.

The bishop waved again – a little shyly, I thought. Pastor Böhm stepped forward to greet him. Next to come forward was the *adat* chief of Olilit Baru, who put his hand upon the bishop's head and prayed to the ancestors, asking for their blessing upon the visit. On that particular day in Tanimbar, God and the ancestors faced each other eye to eye, through the medium of their earthly representatives and, whatever their differences, they found themselves at peace.

When the blessing was done, the Bishop and the Dutch priest made their way to the little Suzuki truck. The bishop climbed on board. Pastor Böhm stood beside him. The truck wobbled a little as the driver switched on his engine.

At this point, things became complicated. A convoy of cars had come from Saumlaki to greet the bishop but, given the size of the crowds filling the area around the airport, the cars could not turn round, and so now the road back into town was blocked by traffic.

The Saumlaki police, armed with bamboo batons, tried to bring a measure of order to things. They shouted and rattled their batons on the trunks of cars, the crowds surged to and fro, the cars revved their engines and the drivers shouted and blew their horns. All the while, the musicians in the pipe bands from Wowonda and Ilngei played their rival tunes, and the bishop stood patiently on his ceremonial vehicle, beaming with unruffled benignity, waving at the crowd. By his side, Pastor Böhm looked strained.

At last the blockage was cleared, and the triumphal procession moved off at walking pace. I joined the crowd ahead of the bishop, a river of people carrying an Episcopal boat to its safe moorings in the church at Olilit Baru. On the verges, more schoolchildren cheered and waved their flags. The pipes and drums descended deeper and deeper into cacophony, attempting unsuccessfully to reconcile the twin demands of playing and marching in procession. Old women, dressed in their finest sarongs, danced in celebration as they walked, their arms extended like noble frigate birds circling on the breeze – the way people danced in olden times. The way that Atuf danced with Inkelu, before time itself began.

The ceremonial boat came to anchor by the church in Olilit Baru, where the bishop said mass for the benefit of the crowds.

That evening, the sounds of pipes continued far into the night. Sometime long after dark, the pipe bands stopped piping and fell to drinking. The people of Wowonda and the people of Ilngei – always natural enemies – fought and squabbled between themselves.

The following morning, Suster Astrid was hard at work in the hospital in Saumlaki, patching up the bloodied, hung over revellers of the night before.

✕

As I made my preparations for departure, my thoughts turned increasingly towards home. I spent my last full day in Saumlaki doing the rounds of friends, saying goodbye, wishing people well.

On that final evening, I took a walk through the Yamdena Plaza, and headed down to the end of the jetty to watch the sunset. The evening was a glorious one, flooded with spectacular yellow light. The sea eagles were soaring, riding the thermals. There was a stiff, warm breeze, and the water was vibrant in the sunlight. Out at sea, I could see the shark boats travelling south in convoy for their night-time poaching in Australian waters, leaving dark wakes behind them.

As I sat there, I heard a voice calling my name. Looking around, I saw a young girl, the daughter of a family I knew quite well. She was about twelve, good in school and intelligent. She had an air of seriousness to her.

'Hello,' she said.

'Hello.' We shook hands. 'How are you?'

She shrugged, looking troubled, and sat down next to me. 'You are leaving Tanimbar?' she asked.

'If there is a plane tomorrow, yes,' I said.

'Will you come back?'

'I don't know. Not for a long time, I think.' I could hear other children, more carefree, screaming as they jumped off the end of the jetty.

She looked down at her feet, and was silent for a long while. 'I have bad dreams,' she said, unexpectedly.

'What kind of dreams?' I asked.

'Frightening ones.'

'I used to have bad dreams,' I said, thinking that this might comfort her. 'I still do sometimes.'

'I don't mean that kind of dream,' she told me. 'I have those as well, but the dreams I am talking about are different.'

'Some of the dreams I used to have were pretty bad.'

'These,' she repeated firmly, 'are different.'

There was something uncannily assured about her. 'How are they different?' I asked. The string of fishing boats was disappearing rapidly southwards.

'It scares me,' she said. 'I dream of bad things happening to people. And when I dream about bad things happening to people, they die.'

'They die?'

She nodded. Her expression was utterly serious. I did not know what to say to her. She sat there, and I could see tears welling in her eyes. 'Do you believe me?' she asked.

'Perhaps, yes,' I said, wishing I knew what to think and what to say.

'You don't think it is my fault, do you?'

'Your fault that the people you dream about die?' I asked.

She nodded again.

'No,' I told her. 'I don't think it is your fault.'

'Nor do I,' she said, 'but it still scares me.'

'I can understand that,' I said.

Then, very grown-up, she put out her hand. I shook it. 'Goodbye, Mister,' she said. 'I hope you visit us in Tanimbar again.'

I said goodbye, and she walked back down the pier alone. When it was dark, I returned home too.

☿

On the morning of my departure, I woke with a thick and sluggish head. My body felt strangely heavy. I sat up in bed, shivering, wrapping my sarong more closely around me. I felt horribly cold. Outside, the weather was oppressive, the sky grim with a brownish cloud and the wind restless and unpredictable. There was an unpleasant stickiness to the air.

I went to have a wash. As the cold water touched my skin, I shuddered. Something wasn't right. I felt as if I had drunk a whole bottle of palm-wine the night before.

I had my breakfast as usual, seated at the bare wooden table as chickens pecked around my feet. After breakfast, feeling dizzy, I lay down again, and I slipped for another hour into strange, confused dreams. I was woken by the sound of Benny knocking on the door.

I sat up and called out, 'Come in!'

Benny came into the house. I swung my legs over the side of the bed to sit up. My head was spinning.

'So,' he said, 'you are off today.'

I rubbed my eyes. 'Yes, I suppose I am.'

'You don't look well,' he said.

'No, I don't feel well.' It still seemed very cold. Looking out of the window, the wind was tearing at the tops of the trees. 'Do you think there will be a flight in this weather?'

'Maybe not. It doesn't look good.'

'How about coffee?' I suggested, thinking caffeine might help.

We drank a cup of coffee together. The caffeine revived me a little, clearing my head. When we finished our coffee, I packed my things.

Then I went to find Ibu Neli, and told her I was ready to leave. She said she would accompany me to the airport.

'Suster Astrid will come,' she said. 'We'll go together.'

Suster Astrid turned up a bit later with a small minibus, and we piled in to head to the airport. By now I was feeling a bit better, but felt apprehensive about the flight. The wind continued to get stronger.

Not long after we arrived at the concrete shack that stood beside the airstrip, and the gloomy promise of the sky was fulfilled. The weather broke into a fierce downpour. We ran for cover, shutting the doors of the building to keep out the torrential rain. Inside it was cramped, with the smell of too many bodies in too small a space. Through the window I could see the runway under a white haze of spray as raindrops exploded on the tarmac. The coconut palms on the other side of the runway were being violently tossed about by the force of the gale. Water started to seep under the door.

I caught the attention of one of the airline officials. I knew him by sight, so I went over and leaned on the counter. 'Are you sure there will be a flight today?' I asked, trying to sound nonchalant.

He opened his eyes wide. 'Why not?' he asked.

'Well, in this weather... won't the flight be cancelled?'

The man gave a reassuring smile. 'Of course the flight will come, Mister William,' he said. 'Do not worry about the weather. I know the pilot personally. He is very brave.'

I felt my skin go cold. 'Brave?'

'Oh, yes,' said the official soothingly. 'In weather like this, many other pilots would have turned back. But not this one. This pilot is a man who does not know the meaning of fear.'

I gave a wan smile. The official, happy he had calmed my anxieties, wandered off to supervise a train of dripping porters who had just appeared with a pile of boxes, laden with fruit.

Ж

The rain eased and the aircraft appeared in the sky – a ludicrously frail little speck, shrouded in glowering cloud. It circled above us, bucking and protesting in the wind. The crowd surged to the window of the shack to watch the descent. Bravely, the little aircraft battled its way out of the air and down to land.

'See?' said the official. 'There really was no need to worry.'

The new arrivals stepped out of the plane and ran across the tarmac to take shelter in the airport building. I chatted to them whilst they waited for their luggage – there were a couple of Chinese traders, a government official, some university-educated Tanimbarese coming home to see their families in the villages, and a pair of bewildered Westerners, still pale and nervous from the flight. But after they picked up their luggage they were gone, hustled into the minibuses and taxis that were waiting to speed them into town.

When the call for my flight came, the weather had begun to turn. The rain had almost ceased, although the wind was still fierce. A brief glint of sunlight flashed on the fuselage of the plane. I said goodbye to everyone, clasping hands with Suster Astrid, and with Benny, and with Ibu Neli. Then I walked across the sodden tarmac towards the plane.

Once in my seat, I looked out of the window back at the airport buildings. I strapped myself in, and the crew closed the doors. The propellers started up, and we rattled down the runway, becoming shakily airborne. The propellers fought against the wind as we gained in height and Tanimbar fell away beneath us. For a few moments I could see all of Saumlaki spread out below me: the pontoon at the back of the Harapan Indah, the jetty stretching out into the bay from the Yamdena Plaza and the church at Olilit Baru. Then, after another few seconds, the plane jolted and we passed through bank after bank of low cloud.

We rose into the sunlight. The temperature in the cabin dropped.

I shivered. My sickness started to return. The door to the cockpit was open. I could see the pilot and the co-pilot chatting. They were beginning to relax. The wind was steadier up here. The pilot opened a newspaper, spread it in front of him, and in this way – with our pilot giving half his attention to piloting the plane, and half to the latest news – we made our slow way back to Ambon.

18

A QUESTIONABLE ENTERPRISE

By the time we landed in Ambon, the shivering was uncontrollable. When I got to my feet, I found that I could hardly walk. I swayed, my vision blurred, I had to hold on to the back of the seat to steady myself. Something, I didn't know what, was very wrong. I took my bags, flopped into a taxi and headed towards town. When I reached the city centre, I caught a bus up to the end of the road where the path into the forest led to Paay and Tin's house.

I staggered down the path that led to my friends' little paradise in the forest. My backpack felt heavy. I had Damianus's sculptures under my arm. I had to stop repeatedly to steady myself and catch my breath. By the time I reached their house, I was pouring with sweat, woozy and sick. Paay and Tin greeted me, looking at me anxiously, then they sat me down and made me tea.

'I'm ill,' I said.

'How long have you been ill?'

'Since this morning. I woke up like this.'

Tin heated up some water to soak some towels. She asked me to take off my shirt, and she draped the hot towels around my shoulders to bring out the fever. My skin was sensitive to the touch, but I was grateful for Tin's careful common-sense approach to medicine – no *sawang*, no *masuk angin*, no *suangis*.

I drank a little tea and ate a few crackers. Then I went to lie down.

I slept for the rest of the day. All night I had jumbled, confused dreams. The following morning, when I woke, the purple bed sheets smelled of rancid sweat, and I was sunk in a thick, heavy fever. I went down to the stream at the foot of the hill and washed away the staleness of a night's sickness. The water was cooling and it revived me a little. But when I came back up the hill to eat, I couldn't keep any breakfast down. Tin kept applying the hot towels. Paay cracked jokes to cheer me up. But all I wanted to do was sleep some more.

A few days later, when there was no sign of any recovery, Paay and Tin took me to the hospital in town. I stood in line outside a complex of low whitewashed concrete buildings and wrote my symptoms on a slip of paper. I passed the paper through a hatch in the wall. A few minutes later, another slip emerged from the same hatch, with a list of medicines and a sum in rupiah. I passed the money back in the other direction and, in a few moments, two bottles of pills appeared in the hatch.

'*Terima kasih*,' I said to the hatch. *Thank you.*

The hatch did not reply. A hand appeared and snapped it shut.

Over the days that followed, the fever came and went in waves. The tides of the fever pulled back for a while, then they rushed in again. Sometimes I was well enough to sit up and talk or read. One day I even took the bus down into town, to run a few errands, but the following night I was raving and delirious again.

I wanted to get better. I wanted to be back on my feet, so I could spend my last month in Indonesia with friends, relaxing, visiting their relatives. I wanted to be no longer stealing with the eyes but simply enjoying people's company, eating, drinking, talking. But I was not getting any better. I was hardly eating anything at all, and I was losing weight fast. Paay and Tin were increasingly concerned.

Then, one day, they came to sit by my bed and said to me, 'You must go home. You are ill. We are worried you are getting worse. Go home to your family. Go home and get well.'

They were right. It was time to go home.

☧

A couple of days later, Paay and Tin accompanied me into town by bus. I was going through a relatively lucid period, and the fever was temporarily in retreat. Taking advantage of this fact, I went to a travel agency and bought a plane ticket to Jakarta. The plane was due to leave the following afternoon.

We caught the bus back up to the forest, and there I slept. The next morning I packed my bags. We got a lift to the airport from one of Paay's relatives. Paay and Tin saw me off. We stood beside the runway, and then the call came to board the plane. I hugged them goodbye.

'Come back soon,' they said. 'Come back, and next time make sure that you bring a wife with you.'

I told them that I'd do my best, and then walked across the tarmac to board the half-empty flight. I put Damianus's sculptures in the overhead locker and took my seat.

We flew back to Jakarta, routed via Sulawesi, arriving before dark. I got a taxi into the city and checked into a dirt-cheap dorm on Jalan Jaksa. I was low on cash, low on energy and low on enthusiasm. I felt emptied out.

That night I went out for a drink with an Australian lawyer. She had recently arrived in the country, having fled the legal profession, and I realised distractedly that I was slightly in love with her. We drank beer and ate *gado-gado* and I told her about Tanimbar, and she told me about where she was thinking of going next, and I fell more deeply in love, and then I said good night to her and, feeling slightly better about life, returned to the dorm to get a good night's sleep.

☧

The following morning I booked a flight home. The women in the travel

agency fed me doughnuts and giggled at my strange Indonesian, pep-
pered with the dialect of Maluku. I put the flight on my credit card, and
resolved to sort out the financial mess I was in when I got home.

A couple of days later, I caught a taxi back to the airport to board my
flight to London. Throughout my stay in Jakarta, the fever had kept its
distance, although I had still been tired and low on energy. As I passed
through customs, an official called me to one side and asked me to open
up the packing around Damianus's sculptures. I undid the cardboard,
and dried grass spilled out. He looked at the sculptures closely, to make
sure they were not national treasures. Then he smiled at me.

'Beautiful sculptures,' he said. 'Where are they from?'

'Tanimbar,' I said.

'Tanimbar is a long way away,' he said. He wished me a good flight
and helped me tie the sculptures back up in their cardboard tubes. He
waved as I headed to the departure lounge.

As I waited for my flight, I wandered the duty-free shop. It was filled
with knock-off copies of Tumburese sculptures, factory made in Jakarta.
'Traditional art from Tumbur,' read the sign. They were both badly
made – pale reflections of Damianus's art – and shockingly expensive.

I arrived home sometime in April 1995. There was nobody to meet me at
the airport. I felt as if I were adrift, as if Tanimbar had hollowed me out,
as if I had no weight to me. I headed back up north and moved in with
friends. For the first few weeks after getting back, the fever came and
went. By the end of the month, it seemed to have more or less abated.

Shortly after my return, I found out that I had secured a funded place
to study for a postgraduate degree in anthropology at the University of
Durham. I would be beginning in September – but that was a long way
off. Until then, being more or less penniless, I took a job in London as a

charity fundraiser. I knocked on doors, asking for donations. I paced the streets of North London – Hampstead, Tufnell Park, Angel – feeling empty and isolated. I was a terrible fundraiser. My heart wasn't in it.

When autumn came, I headed to Durham with a new sense of purpose. I rented a room out of town, set up Damianus's sculptures – totems to watch over me – on a table in the corner, and plunged into the study of anthropology. I spent hours in the company of Bronisław Malinowski, Marcel Mauss, the Nuer and their cattle, the Azande and their witchcraft. And in the company of my fellow anthropologists – all of them professional strangers – I began to feel a sense of kinship. I began to feel at home. Nevertheless, I could not shake the sense that there was something wrong, something out of joint. There was an undertow of unease that I couldn't quite place.

Then the fever started to return.

It returned not all at once, but instead in bouts and fits and stages. I felt the first tremors in the early autumn. One bright October day, as I was walking by the river, I started to shiver. I had to sit down on a bench to recover. There was no wind, but I was cold. The fever came and went in a quarter of an hour, but it left me with a sense of unease that lasted for the rest of the week. Then I had another bout in December, longer this time. I spent two days in bed, wrestling with tangled dreams. The smell of sweat on my bed sheets was a smell I knew from Indonesia. I was about to go to the doctor, but then I recovered. I tried to forget about it.

Then, the following April, I was knocked out for a week. I couldn't walk, couldn't move, couldn't eat. I just sat in a chair, staring into space, shivering and sweating. A friend took me to the doctor. They did blood tests. The doctor asked: had I had sex in Indonesia? No. Drugs? No. Had I been injected? I told him about the nun and her syringe, but said I had fought her off. Had I been bitten by mosquitos? Yes, by hundreds, every day. Did I always make sure to drink clean, boiled water? No, hardly ever.

The doctor made humming noises and referred me to a tropical medicine specialist. They tested me for everything. HIV, malaria, hepatitis. All came back negative. They said I had mild anaemia. They said that the fever looked serious, but they didn't know what it was. I had the unsettling sensation that I was becoming more medically interesting by the day.

After another bout in the autumn, I returned to the tropical medicine clinic, and the doctor looked me in the eye.

'We don't know very much,' he confessed. 'There are so many illnesses that we don't know about. So, tell me – what do *you* think is wrong with you?'

For some reason, I told him about the *sawang*, the stomach-octopus, witchcraft and exorcism and *masuk angin*.

When I had finished, the doctor laughed. 'It could be any one of those things,' he said. 'My guess would be malaria, but you're not testing positive, which is weird.' Then he sat down and took off his glasses. 'Look, do you want my professional opinion?'

'Go on,' I said.

'My professional opinion is this,' he said. 'You are seriously ill, but God alone knows what's wrong with you. So get lots of rest. Forget about all these tests. Come back if it gets worse. And just hope for the best.'

I found ways to make peace with this recurrent fever. I completed my master's degree and started on a PhD. I moved up to Newcastle, just to the north of Durham, to live with friends. I switched my allegiance from Indonesia to India, because I felt uneasy about heading back to Tanimbar. I started to learn Marathi, without any great success. I applied for an Indian visa. And whilst I waited for the bureaucratic wheels to turn, I set about reading books on caste and religion and Indian history.

Some weeks, I was incapable of doing much, but most of the time it didn't worry me. I was getting used to the sickness, finding a way of accommodating myself to its presence. But then, one day in spring, almost exactly two years after I had woken up that final morning in Olilit Baru with a heavy head and a sense of nagging unease, something happened.

It started with a strange gloom that I could not shake off. The gloom shadowed me for days, and there was nothing I could do to shift it. I could feel it sitting there, immovable, somewhere in the base of my stomach. I tried to keep busy, thinking that if I kept myself occupied I might outrun it, but it did not go away. I felt as if something were brewing, something big. I felt as if there were storms on the way.

I was scared.

One afternoon, the gloom became so overwhelming I couldn't ignore it any longer. It was vast and dark and heavy. It wasn't going anywhere.

I put on a CD, lay down on the floor and closed my eyes. It was Sibelius's first symphony. I listened to the swelling harmonies and I started to sob. Once I'd started, I couldn't stop. I sobbed right through the andante and on through the scherzo and the finale, and all the time I had absolutely no idea what was wrong. Grief and sadness broke over me, and I had no idea where it was coming from or what it was about. I thought I was going mad. I thought of that young man in Alusi Krawain whose family had sold the heirloom gold. I thought of failed *adat* transactions, the trail of broken relationships I had left behind in Tanimbar – with Matias, with Abraham. I thought about how I had gone to Tanimbar, two years before, to steal with the eyes. And I was sick of everything: of anthropology, of Tanimbar, of this recurrent fever and, most of all, of myself.

The music came to an end. I heard the CD whirr into silence. I lay there on the floor. The sobbing had stopped. I was glad of that.

When I felt ready, I got up and washed my face. I felt shaky on my legs, but I needed to get out of the house. I crossed the road and cut through onto the path that led along the waterside, past the old warehouses into town. But when I reached the river – broad and brown, swelled with April rain – I had to stop. I was pouring with sweat and shivering. I wondered if I was going to vomit. I could hardly walk. Fever broke over me in waves.

I staggered to the roadside and hailed a taxi to take me home. I stumbled back into the house and vomited. I continued vomiting for the rest of the day and night.

For the next six weeks, I could hardly move. I had no appetite. After climbing the stairs, I would need two hours to recover. Every night I sweated with fever, shivering and trembling. The nausea and vomiting came and went. My friends looked after me with solicitude. The doctors continued to shake their heads. In the daytime I lay on the sofa, too exhausted even to read. I wondered if I was turning to stone, as Atuf had turned to stone, or if I was turning to wood, as Abraham had turned to wood.

I suspended my studies, to give myself a chance to recover. The paperwork was appalling, and I could barely concentrate. It was late May when I sat up and looked at my bookshelves, laden with anthropology books. I looked at Damianus's sculptures sitting in the corner for the room. They gazed back with grave expressions. I thought of Damianus and Abraham and Matias, and I realised that I didn't have the energy to go through all that again, elsewhere, with a different group of people. The problem wasn't Indonesia or Tanimbar. The problem was anthropology. The problem was me. I didn't want to steal with the eyes any more. I wanted out.

I wrote to my supervisor at the university to let him know my intentions. As soon as I did this, very slowly, the fever began to ease. A few weeks later, I took the train to Durham to clear my desk. I had lunch with my supervisor.

'What will you do?' he asked.

'I want to write,' I said. 'I just want to write.' He wished me luck.

It took a while to extricate myself from all my academic obligations. But by the autumn I was free. By this time my Indian visa had come through, but I had no use for it. I sent off emails, cancelled all my plans, gave away my anthropology books. And, as a final act, I donated Damianus's sculptures to the department of anthropology in Durham, to add to their collection. I delivered them in person and handed them over. I hoped that they would like their new home. They were fine sculptures, and they deserved to be looked after. I gave the university a copy of the report I had written in Tanimbar as background, in case future anthropologists wanted to know more about these artworks. Then I went to say goodbye to my fellow anthropologists.

I was sad to leave. But when I caught the train away from Durham for a final time, I felt light and unburdened. My mind was lucid and clear. I had no idea what I was going to do next, no idea where I was going to go. The future was wide open. And, after this great exorcism of hopes and dreams and regrets, I knew that the fever had passed and that it would not be returning.

19

UNFINISHED BUSINESS

Over the years that followed, life took me in different directions: first into the practice of Buddhism, then into philosophy and the writing of fiction. I thought about Tanimbar often, telling and retelling stories to myself and to others. Over time these stories took on a patina, the rough edges worn away – the way that a sculpture, a *walut* perhaps, takes on a rich finish through constant handling – to the point that sometimes I was not sure where the boundary between recollection and fiction lay. I wrote a novel, *Cargo Fever*, loosely based on my experience in Tanimbar. Some years later, I fell into academia again, and started on a PhD in philosophy. I buried myself in Heidegger and Husserl and Levinas. In my thesis, on the topic of stories and ethics, I found myself telling tales about Ubila'a, the supreme deity of the Tanimbarese, about palm-wine and about enchanted pools out in the forests of Yamdena where lovers met with talking fish and found themselves transformed into buffalo. *Barang aneh*. Transformations from the *jaman pertengahan* and the *jaman purba*. Then one day, several years ago, I stumbled across the report I had written after my return from Tanimbar. I typed it up and put it online, because it is still hard to find information about Tanimbar. I hoped it might help somebody or other.

When I remembered Tanimbar, as time went on, it was increasingly with more affection than regret. But I sensed I had some kind of unfinished business there. I was afraid to think too hard about this unfinished business, scared that if I did the fever might return. I had other things to do with my time. I didn't want to get sucked back in.

I took a job at a university. Sometimes, as I sat in my office, I thought back to Tanimbar and there was a shudder in my recollection of this fevered history. I shook off the unease and went back to whatever it was I was doing, subsuming myself in the endless bureaucratic machinery of the university.

But then, almost twenty years after I had left Tanimbar, during a meeting of breathtaking dullness, I received an email from an Indonesian friend. She knew I was interested in Tanimbarese sculpture, she said, and so she was sending me an article she had spotted in the Indonesian newspaper *Kompas*. I surreptitiously opened up the attachment, and I suppressed a gasp of astonishment. In front of me was an image of Damianus Masele, a *walut* in his hand, staring directly at the camera. He looked exactly as he had two decades before, only perhaps a little older. 'Damianus Masele, Defending Tanimbarese Sculpture,' read the headline.

My Indonesian was long rusty from disuse, but, ignoring the meeting that was going on around me, I picked my way through the article. It seemed that since I had left Tanimbar things had not gone well for the carving industry in Tumbur. As the twenty-first century got underway, the bottom fell out of the market and the sculptors in Tumbur drifted back to farming. Of the hundred or so sculptors who were once working in the village, only a handful remained.

In the interview, Damianus talked about palm-wine – it was a sacred drink, he said, but young people did not understand this, and they drank it recklessly – and about carving, and about how the black *kayu hitam* from which the sculptures were carved was becoming increasingly rare. Damianus, too, had gone back to working the land, but he kept his art alive by sculpting in his spare time. 'The craft of Tanimba-rese sculpture,' he said in the article, 'is a heritage from the ancestors that must continue to be preserved.'

He sculpted not because he needed to make a living, nor out of a desire for fame and fortune. Instead, he sculpted because he was an artist. He sculpted because it still mattered.

I got to the end of the article. The meeting droned on around me. I looked out of the window at the grey October sky. Then I wrote to thank my friend in Indonesia, and decided to send another email, to the Department of Anthropology at Durham University, asking whether they still had the sculptures, and whether I could come and visit them. I wanted to pay honour to Damianus's craft, to revisit the two *walut* that he had carved for me. I wanted to make my peace with them. I wanted to make my peace with the past.

It was the following February when I eventually made it up to Durham, travelling with my partner, Elee, who had agreed to act as photographer. When we got off the train in Durham, it was a bright, clear afternoon. There was a bitter wind blowing off the hills. We booked into a bed-and-breakfast room high in the eaves of a house that looked out across the valley towards the cathedral. The view was spectacular, but the wind howled around the roof all night and I slept badly. I felt uneasy at the thought of meeting the two *walut* again.

In the time since I had left Durham, the anthropology department had moved away from the old terrace I remembered, with its meander-ing staircases and eyrie-like offices. Now it was in a newer block up the hill, by the library. Durham had changed since I was there two decades before, but the stolid cathedral, the river that looped through the town and the gaggles of ducks by the weir were all the same.

I had few remaining connections in the anthropology department. People had left, moved on, gone elsewhere. But the departmental technician was welcoming. She let us into the chaotic departmental office and showed us to a desk. The sculptures were laid out ready for us. When I saw them, lying on a bed of bubble wrap, I felt a pang of recognition, recollection and kinship.

Then I noticed something strange about the male figure. Around the neck there was a bandage, and I could see that the head had become severed from the body.

'The head was broken off a few years ago,' the technician told me. 'We're going to ask the archaeologists to reattach it. They know what they are doing. When they've finished their work, the join won't even show.'

Can I pick them up?' I asked.

'Yes, of course,' she said.

I put the two figures upright: the female figure still complete, and the male figure now headless, a loop of white bandage around his neck. Then I picked up his head and held it in my hands.

A severed head. As I held it, it seemed to me as if the final thread that held me to Tanimbar had now been cut. '*Rtetak ulun*', they used to say in Tanimbar: 'they sever the head'.

In all of Tanimbarese art and thought, no image more strongly captures the severing of power or of relationships than the severing of the head. And looking down at the grave and serious face of Damianus's *walut*, it felt as if the strange sway these sculptures and memories held over me was finally done with. But the promise that the head would be reattached was heartening, too. '*Ulur relar ratnemu*', they used to say in Tanimbar: 'the head and neck they join together', a shorthand for the re-establishing of relationships that have been frayed or broken. The promise that the archaeologists would soon join together the head and neck, so nobody would even notice that they had been cut, suddenly seemed less like a repair than it did a reparation. Perhaps, I thought, this was not the end of the story of my relationship with Tanimbar. Perhaps it was the possibility of a new kind of story.

'Can I take the sculptures into the corridor so that we can photograph them?' I asked.

'Yes, do. I'll leave you to it. Give me a shout when you are done.'

We found a place in the corridor where we could rig up a backdrop of sorts and take photographs. I temporarily reaffixed the head with the help of the bandage. We set about stealing with the eyes for one final time, pressing the shutter, taking photograph after photograph of Damianus's artworks. The male figure seemed more co-operative than the female; however skilfully we managed the lighting, she coyly refused to come into sharp focus. But the male figure seemed to appreciate the attention, and responded well to the camera. And although all of this was done without the help of palm-wine, without any prayers offered up to the ancestors, without any proper sense of ceremony, it nevertheless felt like a ritual of sorts – a settling of my debts with the past.

When the ritual was complete, we returned the sculptures to the office. Then, because there was nothing more to be done, we headed back out of the department into the February sunshine, and made our way back down the hill.

Ӿ

When I wake these days from dreams of scattered islands and atolls, rocky bluffs and cliffs that plunge down into the blue-green water, it is no longer with the same nagging sense of unease. Instead, what remains now that I have come to the end of this account – the end of this *mandi adat*, this trading in things half-remembered and half-forgotten, this squaring of accounts with the past – is gratitude. When it comes to the art of exorcism, there is no greater spell than gratitude.

I went to Tanimbar all those years ago to make myself an anthropologist, to steal with the eyes like so many anthropologists before and since. But if Tanimbar taught me anything, it was that the threads of power are more tangled and tightly bound than they first appear. During those months that I lived in the company of sculptors who carved in stone and wood, slowly and patiently – and without my knowing – Tanimbar carved me. It refashioned and remade me in ways that eventually put paid to my relationship with anthropology, this queasy enterprise at the tag end of colonialism. It is thanks to my time in Tanimbar that I found myself eventually heading down new paths, as a sculptor of sorts myself, but one who worked in words rather than in wood and stone, fashioning stories and tales from fragmented dreams, recollections and imaginings.

I used to think that I would never return to Tanimbar. But these days I am not so sure. Sometimes I find myself idly looking at flight schedules, imagining myself walking again up the coast roads, drinking palm-wine in villages at night, trading tales on board the rickety trading ships that shuttle between the outlying islands.

This desire to return has taken me by surprise. It is not a wish to reclaim a lost world. Much has changed since I left. Tanimbar is not the place it was, nor am I the person I used to be. Abraham and Matias, who taught me so much, have almost certainly already joined the ranks of the ancestors. Damianus – consummate artist that he is – still carves in wood when he can, although the rewards are few. My host in Olilit Baru, Ibu Neli, died of stomach cancer in a hospital in Java a few years ago. I am still in touch with her son, Lucky. As for many of my other friends from Tanimbar – Suster Astrid, Benny Fenyapwain, Ibu Lin and Bapak Rerebain – I do not know how they have fared over the past two decades.

My desire to return is not the hope that I might somehow be able to recover the past. Instead what preoccupies me is the fantasy, one day, of returning to deliver this book into the hands of those I knew, or into the hands of their descendants.

As a fantasy, I know that this is vain and self-serving. And yet it is not only these things. For although I was only in Tanimbar for a short while, and never really understood how to play the system, I like to imagine, or at least to hope, that the book might be accepted in the spirit in which it is offered: as a gift. And I like to hope that this two-decade-long exchange of sorts, of gift and counter-gift, might for all its flaws at last be deemed 'tasty', and worthy of the ancestors.

GLOSSARY

The following glossary defines unfamiliar terms in the text, most of which are in Indonesian.

Terms marked with an asterisk (*) come from indigenous Tanimbarese languages, and therefore cannot be found in most Indonesian dictionaries. Most ritual terms in use across Tanimbar are drawn from Fordatan rather than the Yamdenan language. For Fordatan/Yamdenan terms, I have referred to Susan McKinnon's superb book, *From a Shattered Sun*.

adat Ritual law and tradition
Bapak 'Mr'. Term of address to older men
barang aneh Literally 'strange things', used in Tanimbar to refer to a wide range of phenomena associated with ancestors, witchcraft, etc
cuci tanah Literally 'cleaning the earth'. In Tanimbar, this refers to the practice of burning patches of forest to 'clean' them, ready for planting new crops.
curi mata 'To steal with the eyes'
gado-gado Salad consisting of raw and cooked vegetables, sometimes with tofu, served with a peanut sauce
halus Fine, refined
Ibu 'Mrs', term of address to older women
jaman moderen 'Modern era', used by Matias Fatruan to indicate the contemporary or modern world, presumed to begin in the early twentieth century with the coming of the Christian missionaries

jaman pertengahan 'Middle era', the time of the ancestors and the traditional Tanimbarese past, according to Matias Fatruan's scheme

jaman purba 'Ancient era', the third era identified by Matias Fatruan, roughly corresponding to Tanimbarese pre-history and associated with the time before the coming of Atuf

kayu hitam 'Black wood', used to refer to the form of deep brown ebony used to produce carvings in the village of Tumbur

kekuatan mata rumah 'Power of the household', a power associated with a particular household that is considered to be a gift given by the ancestors

kelompok A group or collective, used in Tumbur to refer to the organisation of sculptors into work groups

kmena* Gold earrings, considered to be feminine, Fordatan in origin

kora ulu* Carved prow board of a boat, Yamdenan in origin

loran* Gold earrings, considered to be masculine, Fordatan in origin

main nakal Literally 'to play with wickedness', an expression used commonly in Tanimbar to talk about the performance of black magic

mandi adat 'Ritual law bathing', a term used to refer to a ritual used to 'cool' a sculpture hot with the power of the ancestors

manminak* 'Tasty' or aesthetically pleasing, equivalent to the Indonesian term *enak*, Fordatan in origin

masuk angin Literally 'wind has entered', a commonly recognised ailment across Indonesia

merah-putih 'Red and white', a name for the Indonesian flag

nangin, nangin, o!* 'A story, a story, O!', a traditional Yamdenan exclamation to begin folk tales

natar* A Yamdenan term to indicate the 'stone boat', the ritual centre of the village

orang bule Literally "albino', used to refer to white Westerners

Pak Abbreviation of **Bapak** (see above)

patung mandi Literally 'bathroom sculpture', a sculpture that has been left in the washroom for several years to develop a patina that may make it seem like an antique

rtetak ulun* 'They sever the head'. In the past this Fordatan expression referred both to headhunting and to the rituals surrounding the cutting of elephant tusks to make heirloom valuables.

sasi* A form of *adat* (see above) common across Maluku, concerned with community management and the stewardship of resources, not in general use beyond Maluku

sawang* A stomach ailment, recognised across the Maluku region

sopi Palm-wine

sori luri* Literally 'the bows of the boat', the village ritual official who is considered to stand at the head of the village, just as the bows stand at the head of the boat, Yamdenan in origin

suangi* Common term for a witch across Tanimbar, equivalent to *iwangi* in the Fordatan language. The term is also widely used in West Papua.

tavu* Tanimbarese house-altar, Fordatan in origin

tetek-nenek-moyang Literally 'breast-grandmother-ancestors', the usual term in Tanimbar for referring to the ancestors as a general group. Although the term is Indonesian, as far as I am aware, it is not widely used outside of Maluku and West Papua.

Tuan Honorific form of address, roughly equivalent to 'Sir'

ulur relar ratnemu* A Fordatan-language expression translated by anthropologist Susan McKinnon as 'the head and neck they join together'. This refers to a form of gift given during the negotiation of marriage ceremonies.

walut* A Fordatan term, commonly used across Tanimbar, for a carved ancestor figure. Ancient *walut* are often considered to contain a dangerous 'heat' or power.

ACKNOWLEDGEMENTS

This book has taken an unusually long amount of time to write, and along the way I have accumulated an unusually long series of debts. I would not have made it to the Tanimbar Islands were it not for a generous Bartlett Travel Scholarship from the University of Newcastle upon Tyne. I also received funding from the Sir Philip Reckitt Educational Trust, the Lady Elizabeth Hastings Charities and the Newcastle University Exploration Council.

In Indonesia, I was grateful for the support of the Bapak Rektor Mus Huliselan at University of Pattimura, Ambon, and the Indonesian Institute of Sciences, LIPI. I was so well looked after in Indonesia that I cannot possibly thank everybody, but I'd like to in particular express my gratitude to the following: Damianus Masele, Matias Fatruan and Abraham Amelwatin, who shared their understandings with me; Benny Fenyapwain, for wonderful conversations and substantial insights; Pastor Kees Böhm, for his logistical support; Andrea Flew, for her companionship whilst in Saumlaki; Ibu Neli Batmomolin and her son Lucky, for their generous hospitality in Olilit Baru; Paay and Tin Suripatty, fine and generous hosts; Ibu Lin and Bapak Rerebain, for cures, monumental generosity, many eggs and some impressive dancing; the Malinda family in Sera, for putting up with me; Ronny Fordatkosu, for good jokes, wonderful guitar playing and further practical advice; Dina Go and family, for hosting me in the Harapan Indah; and Suster Astrid, for her relentless good cheer.

I cannot overstate my debt to Susan McKinnon's beautiful and insightful *From a Shattered Sun: Hierarchy, Gender, and Alliance in the*

Tanimbar Islands. It is one of the finest, most subtle and most provocative anthropology books I have ever read. It has shaped not only how I have come to understand Tanimbar, but also how I have come to understand life more broadly.

More recently, I have to thank Grace Susetyo for sending me a timely article about Tanimbarese sculpture from out of the blue. I'm grateful also to De Montfort University for the small research fund that helped me return to Durham as a part of my research towards this book, and to the Department of Anthropology at the University of Durham.

Marilyn Malin and Stephanie Steiker provided guidance and advice on earlier drafts of the manuscript. Portions of the book were also published, in different forms, in *Aeon* and *Unmapped* magazines. I must also thank Haus Publishing for their enthusiasm in shepherding this project to publication. Finally, my gratitude must go to Elee Kirk, for her love, intelligence and sharp wit, and for taking the only two good photographs in this book. Elee heard me tell and retell stories about Tanimbar countless times. Because she did not live to see the book completed, she is now amongst the ancestors to whom this work is dedicated.